*HOW
TO PLAY
WITH YOUR
CHILDREN
(And When Not To)*

HOW TO PLAY WITH YOUR CHILDREN *(And When Not To)*

BRIAN and SHIRLEY SUTTON-SMITH

Illustrations by Daniel Gildesgame

HAWTHORN BOOKS, INC.
PUBLISHERS/New York

Library of Congress Catalog Card Number: 73-339

ISBN 0–8015–3685–5

5 6 7 8 9 10

To our children,
Katherine,
Mark,
Leslie,
Mary,
and Emily,
who played the leading roles
in most of the games
described here

Contents

Contents

Acknowledgments

Investigators whose research on play has made an important contribution to the ideas in this book are Erik Erikson (Stockbridge, Mass.), Jean Piaget (Geneva, Switzerland), Daniel Stern (Columbia Presbyterian Hospital), Burton White (Harvard University), Daniel Berlyne (University of Toronto), Michael Lewis (Educational Testing Service), John Watson (University of California), Alan Sroufe (University of Minnesota), George Rand (University of California at Los Angeles), Dina Feitelson (Tel Aviv University), Sara Smilansky (Tel Aviv University), Erving Goffman (University of Pennsylvania), Edith Kaplan (Clark University), Greta Fein (Yale University), Ruth E. Hartley (University of Minnesota), Gilbert Lazier (Florida State University), Jerome Singer (Yale University), Rosalind Gould (New York University), Iona and Peter Opie (Hants, England), Bernard De Koven (Antioch College), Catherine Garvey (John Hopkins University) Frank Barron (University of California at Santa Cruz), Barbara Kirschenblatt-Gimblett (University of Texas), E.K. and P. Maranda (University of British Columbia), Mihaly Csikszentmihalyi (University of Chicago), and Lois Bloom, Beatrice Beeby, Craig Peery, Beverly Elkan, Amy Miller, June Goldin, Linda Mack, Cornelia Brunner, and Mary Savasta (Teachers College, Columbia University).

We also thank the pupils of P. S. 3 in Manhattan who under their principal, John Melser, are sufficienlty free in their school that they can play with story writing. We have included several of their stories. Special thanks to Alexandra Eldred, Colin Morris, and Jon Vercesi.

The person who convinced us that we had a "message" we should write about was Ben Patrusky. It is entirely possible that he was only being playful.

**HOW
TO PLAY
WITH YOUR
CHILDREN
(And When Not To)**

1 | Why Bother?

REASONS FOR PLAY

Why bother with play? The main reason is that life is generally dull. Often it is downright boring. Anything that makes life a little more interesting is an improvement; and if it makes life exciting, that is a special event.

So, if we do no harm to anyone else and if we do some good to ourselves, then our lives seem more worthwhile. Play makes us enjoy being with each other a lot more. It makes us think life is a little more worth living. As such, play is a rare and life-giving feast. That is why we should bother with it—at least that is the main reason.

So why do we need any more play? It would make life more interesting. You may say that children first have to learn how to work; and, furthermore, you may be too busy to show them how to play. If they watch you, they will see how to work.

But work is not what it used to be. For most people work is not carpet weaving or cattle herding or road shoveling any longer. Work is going in to an advertising agency, a marketing research company, or a classroom and coming up with a new idea. To be successful in the modern world, to keep up with the enormous amounts of new information, and to try to handle the new ways of life thrown at you by a changing society, you have to be versatile. You have to be able to create, but you also must be able to adapt to other points of view. The word "versatile" means two things here: creative and flexible. If a person is creative but not flexible, he may put out the wrong product. If he is flexible but not creative, he may know what the smart thing to do is, but he may not be able to produce. A versatile person has both qualities. He knows that tomorrow something might be done differently

4

and that he has to come up with the right answer when that happens.

What do we know about versatile people? We know they are more playful. Stated in another way, playful people are more versatile.

This is a staggering discovery. For centuries we have believed that playful people were wasting their time. They were wasting our time too. There was work to be done on the farm, and there was work to be done in the factories—hard, grinding work. If we couldn't keep slaving sixty hours a week, we could hardly expect to survive. No wonder we were impatient with idlers, jokers, clowns, and players—that is, unless they could turn their clowning into money, unless they could entertain us. And we certainly are hungry for some release from our own dull, routine lives. We spend twice as much money a year on entertainment and recreation as we spend on military preparation. We care twice as much for that relief as we care for national defense.

But automation is changing our lives. The machine has become our slave, and now we can afford to be more interesting people ourselves. We no longer have to be bits of a human machine. Actually, it is not just that we can afford to be more interesting; it is more compelling than that. If we are not interesting, we cannot get a job. If we do not have new ideas about how to make our vast information culture work, we are not of much use.

Every branch of politics, government, business, and education needs versatile people. Everywhere the cry is raised, "If only we had more versatile leadership, if only those at the top could think of new ways of handling old problems, instead of repeating the same mistakes, or making new mistakes. Why can't they come up with answers that will cover all the variables in complex problems?"

This is another reason why we need more play. We know that those who play more are more versatile. We know that versatile people are in high demand and will be in even higher demand in the future. This book is about the production of versatile people.

LEARNING TO PLAY

But, you say, surely children don't have to be taught to play. Play is the one thing they can do for themselves. Surely children play by instinct. It is *not* true that children play by instinct. You have to learn to play.

There are some societies where children hardly play at all. In some societies children's work is so important that they are expected to help from the earliest years. Little two-year-olds sit and watch adults at silk weaving.[1] Four-year-olds carry babies on their hips, while seven-year-olds prepare the meals in earth ovens. In some parts of the world seven-year-olds will spend most of their day looking after the cattle.[2] Both parents may work all day, and yet children's work is also needed if everyone is to have enough food to eat. There is little time for play.

It is true therefore that children learn how to play from others, but we have to admit that there is a *little bit of instinct* in it. No one shows babies how to play during their first few months. Yet they do. They play with their lips. They play with their bubbles. They play with their fingers. They play with their cooing. That much seems to be there at the start. As long as we feed them, as long as we handle them and keep them comfortable, babies do that much for themselves.

1. Dina Feitelson, "Some Aspects of the Social Life of Kurdish Jews," *Jewish Journal of Sociology* 1 (1959): 201–216; and H. Ammar, *Growing Up in an Egyptian Village* (London: Routledge and Keegan Paul, 1954).
2. See for example the Nyansongo of Kenya as described in Beatrice Whiting (ed.) *Six Cultures* (New York: John Wiley, 1963).

But from about three months of age on babies begin to be aware of what others are doing—and they look and look and look. In fact, not only babies, but all children will spend about 60 percent of their free waking time *just staring* during their first six years of life. We adults do a fair bit of it too. We sit on the porch and do it. We do it on the bus. Television has simply made a profit out of our enjoyment of just watching.

In the same way, babies will watch you; and, if you play yourself, they will soon learn to play as well. Most of the play and games of the world have been learned not by teaching but by watching.

To become playful, however, babies must have some play to watch. Naturally it is easier for them to learn from playing with you than from just watching you. We all learn more through doing, even though we can learn a great deal through observing.

PARTICIPANTS IN PLAY

Who is to play with the baby? Fortunately, because your baby wants to play, a little will go a long way. It is the occasional example that counts. In fact, everyone can help, including your nine-year-old and those still younger. A little bribery can add to both their own resources and those of the baby: "A nickle for every new game you can teach the baby." It doesn't take long for the number of games to increase.

Many of us who think we understand the great importance of play as a new way of life were brought up under the old regime. We had parents who worked day and night. We still work fairly hard ourselves. Our hearts may not be fully with our minds, and we may not always do what we know we should, but we can get everyone in the family occasionally involved—mother, father, and older brothers and sisters; and, later, everyone at the nursery school, day-care center, or kindergarten, including the teachers, aides, and students.

If everyone accepts the idea and does a bit of the playing, then that will probably be enough. Babies begin to play themselves and do not need many cues in order to continue or expand their play. Also, you do not have to continue playing night and day. In fact, the ruling principle in this book is, "If it isn't fun, forget it." You only carry on these games if both parties are enjoying it. If one party is tired of the game, then give it up.

This book is about people enjoying themselves together. One of our playful friends says that his rule is more positive than ours. Instead of "If it isn't fun, forget it," he advocates, "If it is fun, foster it, no matter how awful it is." That is something we can assess as we go along, but it at least gets at the spirit of this book. What we need is just enough play in our lives to get our unimaginative souls to take those few steps that will make our own children have better answers to society's problems than we have.

There is still another reason for all this play. The families that are left must count. We are all coming into a world where there are going to be fewer babies and where they will more often exist because their parents wanted to have them. Everything we know about human progress suggests that the most outstandingly talented people came from small families in which they were given a great deal of attention and had a great deal of closeness with their parents. Unfortunately, too much closeness can also lead to neurotic dependency or hostility. Playfulness is one of the ways to ensure that closeness also leaves plenty of leeway for growth. You cannot be concerned about mutual play and solitary play and still retain the old stifling overconcern. Play makes the family and its children a place where there are many joyful occasions and a great deal of fun. Those who remain versatile remain interesting and interested and have no need to stifle each other.

But this kind of play is embarrassing. This is the rub. Making faces, being a clown, playing the fool—why should we do all that? How can we expect to become a flexible rubber-face entrepreneur of funny ideas—galloping around the floor, swinging the baby upside down, talking nonsense to our seven-year-old, playing Frankenstein? No one can expect it. But the message of this book is that playing is such a simple activity that anyone can adapt it to his own family style. Once you have the knack, it is not hard to invent play and games that introduce novelty that your own family enjoys and that fit your own style of embarrassments. This book is meant to set you off on your own tracks rather than to provide a bible of games.

In any case, it is encouraging to know that your best answer to the future of civilization might be on the floor—flat on your back, holding up your one-year-old baby, and making faces at each other.

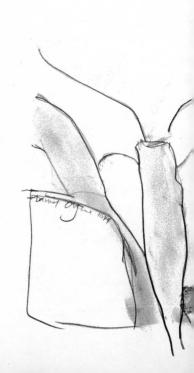

2 On Being A Clown:

From Birth to Three Months

They smile delightedly at their mobiles turning quietly above their heads.

•

She catches my finger as I feed her. I pull it away. She clutches it again. I pull it away.

•

I blow bubbles with my lips in front of his face. He smiles.

•

I rub my head on her stomach. She chuckles.

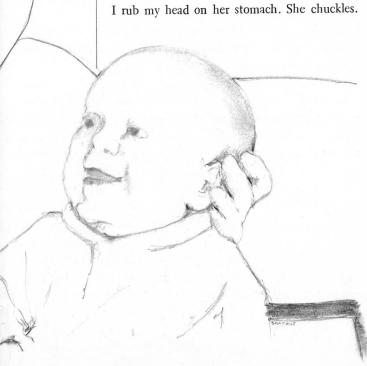

Before you can begin to play with babies, you have to *get in touch*. There has to be some communication. This can begin about the end of the second month, when babies begin to become somewhat more alert to those about them.

The basic rule for getting in touch is to *imitate* them whenever you can. When they smack their lips, then you smack yours. When they snort, snuffle, sigh, gurgle, or breathe heavily, you try to make a sound as close to theirs as you possibly can. It is not easy. But put your face about a foot away from theirs and act like a perfect mimic. For those of you who had a childhood full of finger-popping cheeks, raspberries, and loud clacks of your tongue on the roof of your mouth audible throughout the high school auditorium, this will be an interesting challenge. These sounds represent the beginnings of communication.

Eventually a baby will repeat the sound that you have just imitated. By responding to babies in terms of what they can do, you give them a chance to respond to you with what they have. They make noise, you make noise, they repeat the same noise. That is the first human communication. It is also what education is supposed to be about—that is, using what is already there to make something.

Some mothers are able to play imitating games with their babies by the end of the first month—but not many. Many parents are able to establish these close contacts within three months, however. One must remember that a lot of simple caring must go on to provide a basis for closeness. In the first month of life one may be too exhausted by feeding the baby, by being up every night, by getting over childbirth, by being depressed about recovering your figure, or by paying the doctor's bill to worry about games.

So your first enjoyment will be just the enjoyment of feeding, cuddling, holding, and even the special pleasures of smelling the baby's fresh skin and touching his or her fuzzy head of hair. You begin to discover to what sort of individual you have given birth and to adapt your holding and feeding habits to the baby's needs and temperament. He may be strong and vigorous or mildly active or quiet. He may be irritable or rather easy to live with.

One should not expect early returns. Actually, the baby cannot do much that is visible to us as yet. Although babies are complex systems, they cannot respond very well to us. They have only a few minutes after feeding and before sleeping when they are really alert to the world about them. They stare alertly at large objects, especially bright ones. They take hold of anything we put in their hands to grasp. They may hold their heads up a little, while on their stomachs or backs. But their necks are still very weak and their heads flop over when we are holding them, so they must be cradled in our hand. Their arms wave about fairly wildly when they are not held. But they notice sounds and their directions. They are soothed by rhythmic sounds or movements. They are sensitive to the way they are held, and they can distinguish strong tastes, smells, heat, and cold. In fact, the more we learn about newborn babies, the more we discover what they can already do.

There can be no getting in touch without a lot of care first, however, meaning a lot of cuddling and rocking. We put them in the mood for communication by closeness and acting together. Usually repeated sounds, such as snorts, coos, and snuffles, will be quite clear by the third month, if they have been worked at and if the parent has been playing (that is, imitating) when feeling like it.

We are not just imitating gurgles and snuffles. We must know how to *keep in touch*. By three months, if not earlier, we are undoubtedly *talking* to the baby in that very special way that parents have. Most parents do not like to be told that they do these things. But there are now records on film, taken by Dr. Daniel Stern, of New York, and we know that practically any good parent does it.

Parents talk to their babies and *keep in touch* by *elongating their vowels*: "Hi sweee-e-e-e-t-e-e. Hi-i-i-i-i. Are ya loo-o-o-kin' at Moo-o-meee?" The range of pitch is increased, especially at the high end. (Imagine the above statement in a high squeaky voice.) Speech is slowed down or stretched out. (The hyphens above suggest the process here.)

Their faces assume mock exaggerated expressions. There are raised eyebrows and wide-open eyes, like the made-up faces of clowns themselves or like the clownlike pictures of faces that hold the attention of young infants in the experiments on what babies will look at in the first six months of life. The mouth is also open and pursed in saying "Oooo-oooo." The head comes up and forward to within inches of the baby's face.

Parents gaze into the infant's eyes for a long time. Sometimes they look at each other for more than thirty seconds, which is an unusually long period of time for adults unless they *are* in love. Usually this is a one-sided conversation, with the parent doing all the talking and most of the looking, but, combined with all the other points above, it seems to be what keeps the baby looking at the parent. We should mention too that at two to three months babies gaze at their mothers with complete and total rapture, which we call *eye-love*. Eye-love is beautiful to see, and it is the second form of human rapture. The first form is having a nice warm stomach full of milk.

So we imitate babies to get in touch, and we speak in this odd way to keep in touch. If we don't, they cease to pay attention to us and look somewhere else. The amusing thing is that babies really force us into this behavior. If we do not do it, they will ignore us. We are forced into continually doing something novel, either making faces or sounds, in order to get their attention. Even if we did not want to play, we would have to. As long as we want their attention, we must play.

We have now shown two ways in which you have to be a clown to get in touch and to keep in touch with babies. It might be reassuring for you to know that everyone does it. Better-educated mothers tend to do more of it. Mothers who keep in touch in these ways develop a very good communication with their babies by three months or so. Both mother and baby look at each other and look away from each other at roughly the same time. Mothers and babies who have not paid so much attention to each other tend to have this all messed up. Each one looks when the other is not looking. It is like unrequited love. I am sure we all know a lot of people who do not seem to know when to look and when not to look, even when to gurgle and when not to gurgle. Anyway, this is where it all begins.

GAMES AND OTHER THINGS TO DO

But now let us return to games. We have been dealing with ways to play-communicate with babies and how to continue this activity by being a clown.

The Game of Gurgle

We have already told you about this game, but now we want to make it formal. There are two stages: First stage: one-month-old baby makes back of throat gurgle; parent, leaning close to baby's face, repeats same sound; baby smiles. Second stage: Two-month-old baby gurgles; parent gurgles; baby repeats own gurgle.

Now you are in touch and have the basic elements in a

game, which is two people working together to produce something. But notice, there is always an uncertainty about what will happen. Will you get a gurgle or not? Now clearly babies do not know that they are playing a game in this sense. They only know that they are enjoying themselves. Most of the games that parents play with children are like that. They are sort of one-sided, *except* that both have fun. Also, the baby is being hooked into the system of turn-taking, without which no game (nor for that matter most social life) is possible.

At this early stage there is also something very important to say about *not* playing games. You must always begin those activities that are clearly games quietly and gently. Some babies simply may not want the stimulation yet, or perhaps not at the time you are trying, and they use their one technique for controlling you. They turn away either their head or their eyes. Other babies are more ready, and they respond. You must adjust your energy and pace to the babies' responses.

The Game of Diaper Push

By the second month babies begin to respond to you. When you lift them, they pull with their arms. In the bath they kick the water. They more regularly put new things in their mouths. They turn their heads and eyes toward moving people and blink when people come toward them. Their eyes follow a moving person, although often in a jerky way, like a camera having to refocus at each fixing.

The game of diaper push emerges while you are changing the baby's diaper for the umpteenth time. Lean over the baby and let her push her feet into your stomach. She tends to push harder against you. When pushed, you leap back with the push, crying "Aagh," or whatever your favorite whoop is, but not too loudly. Then push forward on the legs again. She pushes back at you.

The game is actually begun in a milder way than suggested here. First you press very gently down on the baby's feet with your stomach. Then, as you are pushed back, you move backward and then forward again until the infant seems to notice the action and reaction and begins to smile as it is repeated. As the game develops, you can add the antics of leaping backward, and so forth, always remembering that continuing and extending the intensity of a game depends on whether the infant is indeed interested. Fortunately, at this stage there is not much you can do about infants' turning off. It seems to be one of their best defenses against too much stimulation. If they can't use your input, they turn away.

We should add that diapering has become a favorite occasion to move and smile. It is as if this were the first playground, although some authorities feel that the baby's playing with his mother's finger as she feeds him is the first playground. Anyway, diapering is certainly a popular time for play. There are many play activities that can take place while diapering, including gently and rhythmically slapping their little bottoms, tickling their tummies, and playing bicycles with their feet in your hands. Babies' bare nether regions are always inviting.

The Game of Poking Out the Tongue

Toward the end of the second month, but certainly into the third, you are both poking your tongue out at each other (if you've been working at it). There are little smiles of recognition coming your way. We do not agree with those people who say that she will be sticking her tongue out at people for the rest of her life. The evidence suggests that nothing continues throughout life that does not continue to get rewarded, and we are not going to go on rewarding her for this—at least not when we get into some more-sophisticated games.

Dancing

Dancing is not really a game because there is not meant to be any uncertainty, and games are not games without uncertainty. However, because most people are poor dancers and poor coordinators, there often *is* an uncertainty even in dancing. We put dancing here because it is a part of playfulness with children. It is a great deal of fun to dance around holding a little baby in your arms. Jiggle his arm up and down to the music and in time with the rhythm. When you stop or the music stops, he keeps his arm going up and down. It is better to call dancing a *ritual*, because it brings people together. That's what rituals are, activities that bring different people together; for in dancing we are unified.

If you have a large family, then the music sessions around the guitar, the hi fi, or the TV music show can be even more unifying for all family members. Even a small baby seems to feel the excitement of everyone dancing.

There are some social groups where babies are always carried on their mothers' backs and therefore always moving in accord or in unison with their mothers. Because of this the babies show remarkably rapid physical development. They sit up and walk much earlier than do babies in Western civilization, walking as early as eight months, whereas our average is one year.

Still, we are advocating a little rhythm as a game rather than as a way of life. Some strong mothers might try more dancing if they have the energy for it.

Singing

Like dancing, singing can be either a parent and baby activity or an all-family pastime, or both. It can be with piano, guitar, or just a TV commercial or simple folksong. The melody of the song is what keeps the baby's attention (like "sweeee-t-e-e," mentioned earlier). The baby simply "hangs on the song," watching you eagerly throughout. Our favorite, which we must have sung a thousand times, was a sad old children's game called "Green Gravels," which children used to play in the 1800s. The words follow:

> Green gravel, green gravel, the grass is so green.
> The fairest young lady that ever was seen.
> He sent you a letter to turn around your head,
> Oh Mary, Oh Mary, your true love is dead.

The baby was not aware of the morbidity but was attracted, we think, by the simplicity and regularity of the rhythm and melody.

The Game of Biting Parent's Finger

By three months babies have fairly sophisticated mouths, and they can use them only too well. Their eyes now focus on a target quite well. Their neck muscles are stronger, so they can adjust their heads better. There is a great game that you can play from about three to six months, which we call "biting parent's finger." It hurts! In this game the parent slips a finger in and out of the baby's mouth. You win if you slip it in and out again without being bitten. The baby wins if she bites you.

If you are lucky in this early period, the teeth are not developed and you only have to deal with stiff hard gums and a powerful suck. This game, like all others, is helped and aided by mock cries from you, exclamations, and huggings, which communicate the importance and enjoyment of the climaxes. Biting parent's finger is like a real game in that it is organized entirely by the coach (the parent) and there is both a winner and a loser.

The Game of Pulling the Hand from the Lion's Mouth

This is another sophisticated *mouth* game. You chew his hand, very carefully of course. He pulls the hand away, and you put it back; or he pushes it into your mouth, and you nibble it. He pulls it out, then pushes it back again—all with much smiling by both of you. We are not sure, though, that we can trust all adults with this game; little babies are pretty succulent.

The Game of Pinky Pulling

While the mouth is playing some tricks, the hands and arms have also been shaping up. By now babies tend to pull or grasp whatever is in their hands. The game of pinky pulling is a later version of finger biting, and much less painful. By the third month babies begin to reach fairly regularly for things they see, usually with a two-armed pincerlike swipe in the object's general direction. So if you hold a finger up in front of the baby's face, she reaches for it and may grasp it. Then you pull somewhat, and she pulls somewhat. After doing this for a bit, you pull away but then give her the opportunity to grab the finger again. The tugging goes on once more, getting the finger free, having it caught, until she loses interest. This is the first game of tug-of-war.

The Game of Bob-White

By three months also babies are turning their heads in the direction of sounds. They are responding to your talking to them with some babbling of their own. That is, they are "making sounds" rather than just expressing feelings of pleasure and pain (the cries and coos of the first two months). The imitative game they seem to like at this time is an advance on the game of gurgle above. It is the lengthening of a low sound and then adding a quick high sound on the end, as does the bird known as a bobwhite. Babies are clearly capable of changing the length of the "Bob" and thus pacing the surprise ending. There is delight in doing this either with you or by themselves.

Mobiles: Red and Yellow

We have games for the mouth, for the legs, for the hands, and for sounds. We obviously should have a game for the eyes, but we don't. By three months babies are looking more at faces. They seem to recognize you. They look into your eyes as if they have decided the eyes are the important part of the face to look at. They spend much time watching mobiles if there is one hanging above their crib. If you put one up, it should be quite simple—just one object that turns in the breeze, with perhaps a different color on each side. If there is no breeze, slowly alternate the colors. Red and yellow are interesting to babies, but mobiles are not games.

CAVEATS

Things we could tell you, but you should read about in other, more-sober manuals:

Wash your hands before playing bite the finger!

Babies are very different. Some just love these arousing games, others have to proceed at a quieter pace.

Mothers are also very different. They have to explore carefully to see if their babies are like them. Maybe they are not. Maybe they are opposite—mother noisy, baby quiet; baby noisy, mother quiet. You have to reach some compromise there.

Fathers are also very different. Some are straight, some are clowns. Some babies love clowns, others do not appreciate them.

Infants are only good for a few minutes of play per day in the first month or so, then they are off to sleep again. You do not have much time to "work" with.

I suppose we could add our personal view that homes are principally for living in. The place for singing and playing and dancing with the baby is in the nicest and warmest part of the house, which is usually the living room. Activities in a house should be centered primarily around fun and only secondarily around appearances.

THE BABY'S OWN PLAY

In order to be playful you also have to be a good observer. Therefore a large part of this book is devoted to telling you what to look for. Our belief is that by watching what babies are doing, you will be able to invent new ideas for what to do with them. After all, during the first year of life almost anything babies do that can be imitated can become a game. Once you start responding to each other, new sounds and new actions creep in.

Whether or not you play with the baby, he will be playing on his own, although the evidence suggests that, other things being equal, the more you play with him, the more he will play by himself. Children do mainly what those around them do. If the adults in a child's life do not play, the child will not play much either, and they will all have a dull time together.

We should warn you that no matter how much time you put in, it will usually be just a fraction of the baby's free time. It has been shown that babies are on their own while awake, amusing themselves, about 90 percent of the time, and sometimes a great deal more. The mother's total caretaking time is usually less than 10 percent of the baby's waking time.

The manner of play is important to babies just on the basis of time spent. But probably even more than that it is important because that is the only time that the baby (the infant or the child) and the adult are truly free agents. The famous child psychologist Erik Erikson has said that play is what we do with the leeway of experience—that is, with the leftover, free part of experience.

How babies play at first is not easy to observe, but we think that the first examples are *mouth play*. Even in the first months we can observe babies bubbling saliva on their lips and moving their tongues around their mouths. They often seem to be particularly relaxed while doing this. They look as if they are "musing" or "ruminating." We are probably correct in thinking they are at play. That is, they are no longer hungry or uncomfortable. They are no longer trying to discover something or get to something. They are observing what happens when they vary things. They are being versatile with their mouths. Of course this play looks as if it is accompanied by a lot of pleasure. What we may later call the excitement of play, we can at this time call its pleasure.

After mouth play there is *hand play*. The babies hold their hands together or explore their mouths with their forefingers. They are calm and seem to be enjoying themselves, as judged by their coos and their not seeming to want anything in particular. After feeding they run their fingers through the goo of the cereal on and around their lips.

Around the second and third months too there is usually much *sound-making play* (vocal play). They may gurgle with some of the milk in their throats or make throatlike sounds. When we remember that their greatest competence in these first three months is with their mouths, with sucking and swallowing, it is not surprising that this sort of skill is what gets varied in play. At the end of the third month they will probably be talking to themselves, even without others present.

There have been research projects to determine whether babies of this age will use their ability to suck to bring a picture into focus. An apparatus equipped with a nipple is used; if it is sucked in certain ways (arranged by the experimenter), the picture, which is projected on a screen before the babies, will be seen clearly. If they do not suck it just right, the picture goes out of focus. The results have shown that they can do this, they can get the picture into focus, which indicates that they are much more alert to the world around them than we would give them credit for.

Once again though we have had to use their skills (in this case, sucking) as a starting point. The good educator, we repeat, is the person who takes what is there and organizes it. The future of baby toys lies in the hands of those inventors who can make use of this principle. One psychologist has, for example, invented a toy that enables a two-month-old baby, by pushing her head harder on her pillow, to make her mobile move. Basically, the pressure on the air in the pillow exerts air pressure on a trigger that moves the mobile, which is in the baby's line of vision. With toys of this sort babies can gain very early a sense of mastery in a world where they are usually thought of as helpless.

Obviously from our examples we think that you can get in touch with babies and that you can keep in touch with them.

By imitating them you can find ways of having fun together. You should continue to play as long as you are *both* having fun, allowing for both the baby's feelings and your energy level. There are games for sounds, for the mouth, for the hands, and for the legs; and the eyes are always active. In most of these games and other activities you are of course the coach. These games lift babies to a higher level than they could otherwise reach. Just compare the complexity of the games that we have mentioned with the simplicity of the babies' own play that we have described. Your social play provides examples for their future. Later in their own play they will reproduce what you have shown them.

We do not know how you have felt about being a clown through all this. You have used a most peculiar voice. You have been gurgling and popping your lips. You have poked out your tongue. You have been leaping in the air, dancing, singing, getting your finger bitten, and making noises like a bird. There might be those who would want to put you away, but the baby would not.

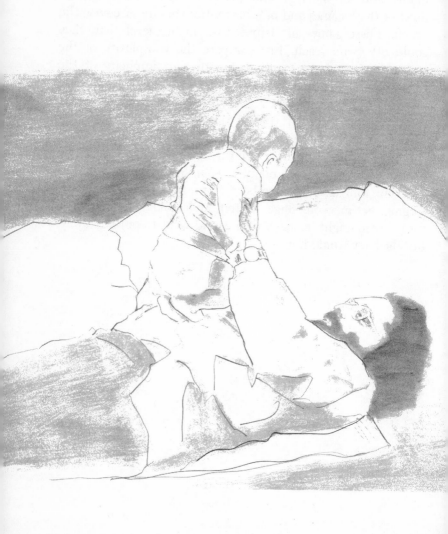

3 The Birth of Laughter:

From Three to Six Months

His chief enjoyment was flipping backward on to the bed.

•

She loved to be dropped and caught again.

•

When one parent was worn out, he loved to do it all over with the other.

By the end of three months we have a real person on our hands. Now babies really look you in the eye. In technical terms their eyes converge on yours. Their looking patterns and yours work together. That is, when they look, you look; when they look away, you look away, etc. Looking at each other is a higher level of communicating. Put another way, after the first three months babies become increasingly directed to the world outside of themselves.

GAMES AND OTHER THINGS TO DO

It is possible that you will not have had much success with the games of the previous chapter—gurgle, diaper push, poking out your tongue, dancing, biting mother's finger, pinky pulling, and pulling your hand from the lion's mouth—until this period. These games usually become more frequent at this time. It is also true that if you have not tried very much to establish such communications during the earlier period, you may not get them very easily now either. But since many parents do begin these gamelike communications in the second and third months, we have listed them there.

Still, from the end of the third to the sixth month is the time when most parents will really begin to have *fun* with their babies, and that is what this chapter is about.

Making Baby Laugh

Babies smile at or soon after birth, but it does not have much to do with you at that time. The smile is just like other forms of restlessness or movement. By about two months babies smile at the objects and the people they recognize. The pictures on the crib and the people in their families will get most of the smiles. Smiling seems to express recognition. Increasingly after three months, however, smiling is done only for people. It has been turned into a social form of behavior. Then comes laughter.

Somewhere between the third and the fourth month you sometimes can get at least a chuckle and, if you are lucky, full-scale laughter by various assaults on the baby's person. What seems to work best is a sudden incongruity or puzzlement for the baby, just as theorists of humor have said. For example, when you are leaning over the baby to look at him or to adjust him in the crib, if you change direction and gently put your head on his stomach instead of looking at him face to face, you can sometimes produce a smile. If you do this again several times, he may laugh.

The principle is that any regular behavior, if varied, can cause laughter. Remember, however, we mean that this happens if it is varied in the familiar situation by familiar and trusted adults. Play and games are a delicate part of life, and they exist well only when we can trust the other players, when we are comfortable in the surroundings and at home with the situation.

The interesting thing for the adult to do is to invent other ways of making the baby laugh. In all cases, again, the principle is simple, to vary your regular behavior with the baby at a time when the baby is very comfortable with you.

You might also try the following: While she is lying on her back being diapered or whatever, pick her up and lower her, bouncing her up and down on the bed a few times. Pick her up by the legs, upside down (gently the first time), and move her up and down. Holding her carefully over the bed and close to it (in case you are not much of a catcher), toss her into the air just an inch or two.

Try sounding out nonsense to him. Babble at him (bobo bo bo bo bo) on a rising crescendo. Make your cheek pop with your finger, if you have the skill. Blow raspberries on his neck or cheeks while he holds your head or hair. Find new places to tickle. For example, when washing him, you may find that the corner of the washcloth tickles the inside of his hand or that it tickles him under the chin.

If you want to think of these things as games in a typical way, keep score on how many different ways you have found to make the baby laugh. But keep it gentle to begin with. As the baby participates and reacts, what you do can be done in larger proportions, louder or faster or with a wilder face. You should always keep an eye on babies, however, to make sure they are not becoming upset.

Look for *surprise* on your baby's face. If she does not act surprised, it may not be striking her as all that funny. It is interesting to watch babies just after you have done one of these unusual things. Sometimes they will watch you alertly, see you smiling, and then smile themselves. At other times their faces may crumple suddenly, and they may look upset. That is the time for a hug and a cuddle and the reestablishment that all is OK. They may not be ready for games today. Perhaps you began too rapidly or too boisterously. Actually, most of these warnings are not necessary. Most parents know their babies well enough to be able to gauge their readiness for more arousal, more or less excitement.

By six months babies' social lives are now sufficiently advanced that if you laugh, they may well laugh with you; if you smile, they may well smile with you. So even without tickles laughter can do the trick by itself. Such laughter on your part may evoke squeals of delight. Babies can also tell what is funny just by looking. They expect to see one thing but see something else. Thus, you can produce a laugh by throwing things or by falling over, as long as these are accompanied by smiles. This means you have moved to laughter that is provoked solely visually.

Although we have been using the license of calling all these activities with infants "games," because that is most often what they are, making the baby laugh is really more like a drama. There is usually a plot to these things. The first time we put our head on their stomachs, they are surprised. The second time, they burst out laughing. And then the next time, as you wag your head around above them, their anticipation builds to the climax. These pieces of theater may be brief, and they involve audience participation (this audience gets directly tickled), but they are drama. In drama the great thing is anticipation and mounting excitement. There is a lot of this in play with babies.

Knee Games

At four months babies can sit up with support, although if you are not very careful, they will flip back and hit their heads on the floor. So you sit them up in pillows, or you buy a jumper chair that holds them up, or you dig a hole in the sand and put their bottoms in it (they are always bottom heavy with diapers anyway), or you sit them cradled in your legs. From that we get the game of knee bouncing. Sitting on your knee, they now spontaneously rock a little back and forth. This produces the possibility, once again, of your imitating them and their imitating you. They rock a little, then you bump your knees up and down (simply lifting the heels up while keeping the toes in place), then they rock a little. This is an alternation type game, in which each takes a turn (as in hopscotch or jacks at a later age).

There are traditional knee games—for example, "Ride a Cock Horse." In this game you cross one knee over the other and perch the baby on your free foot. Hold his hands and jerk your free leg upward and downward rhythmically while you sing the words:

> Ride a cock horse to Danbury Cross,
> To see a fine lady upon a white horse,
> With rings on her fingers and bells on her toes,
> She shall have music wherever she goes.

The baby's eyes will rarely leave your face. He will smile broadly at the end, then jiggle himself up and down, signaling that he wants you to do it again. Oblige him; it is a good exercise for you.

There is a whole category of knee games, because sitting babies on your knee is the most convenient place for doing things together. You can dangle things in front of them, such as a rattle, and have them lunge for the objects. They grab and, of course, suck. Here you can tantalize a little, keeping the rattle out of reach until the best lunge and then letting them have it.

We should warn here, and everywhere throughout this book, that although teasing may be fun to you, it is often plain hostility to somebody else. "I'm just having fun with him," says the mother as she pushes the three-year-old into the sea. "Got to make a man out of him," she explains, while he screams his head off. It is very clear that aggression and hostility toward children are very widespread and that many people disguise this from themselves by saying that they are having fun. Since we have emphasized that everyone have fun, it is important that we dissociate our notion of a game from one-sided teasing of that sort.

This point cannot be stressed often enough. One of the major sources of gratification for many of us, in and out of games, is venting aggression at someone else's expense. And there are indeed places and times for that sort of thing; there are cocktail parties and there are games of football. We would not for a moment take them from those who enjoy them. But it is so easy for that kind of real fun to stray into relationships with children and become justified (in the parent's eyes), because it is so much fun for the parent.

An amusing lap toy is the *mirror*. You hold it, they gaze at it and paw it. We are not sure how early children come to recognize themselves in the mirror, but current research seems to suggest that it is during the first year. Their own picture is much less of a stranger to them anyway than are the faces of other strangers.

From knee games we go to "pretend" standing. You hold babies by their hands, and they stiffen their legs to stand up, with a great effort. Next there is "pretend" walking. You hold their hands and they make "steps" along the floor without going anywhere. As an even more exciting form of gymnastics you hold their arms and let them bounce up and down on the bed with stiffened legs, which is a first form of trampoline.

Blowing Bubbles

By the age of four or five months our infants are waking up in the morning and, instead of crying first thing for milk, they are cooing or babbling to themselves, having their own morning talk period. Out of this play they develop a considerable versatility with sound making.

The game of blowing bubbles is not really very different from the first game of gurgle or snuffling at babies. But now you do not have to wait for them to make the sound before you copy them. If you lean over them and make a "raspberry" sound or blowing-bubbles sounds, babies will look at you intently, even perhaps smile. They will then try to make some sound of their own. You can get their attention with these sounds if they are not watching. What they are doing is answering your sounds with their own. Thus the roles are reversed. They are imitating you, rather than you imitating them. By the time they are six months old, you and they can even take turns blowing raspberries on each other's cheeks.

Hair Pulling

From four to six months babies learn to coordinate their eyes, their hands, and external objects. That is, they begin to reach for things when they see them and begin to grasp them. Before that these three abilities—to look, to grasp, and to reach—did not work together. Babies did not reach for what they could see. They did not look at what they grasped in their hands. Now they close in on things with both hands swinging together like Frankenstein. Thus when you lean over and your hair hangs down, they grab at it and pull it. Then, if you are not too busy with the diaper, or perhaps because you are, you pull away, they pull again, you pull away, etc.

Their strong grip, which is good for such games, is good for other things too. When they sit on your lap and take hold of the tablecloth, their strong grip can pull it right off the table. When you are leaning over, they can take your hair or your nose in a very strong grip and, particularly if their fingernails have not been cut recently, give you a healthy scratch.

Singing

Your lullabies or singing or chanting of "commercials," which previously have been woven into your day-to-day routine with the baby, now have a separate and distinctive role. Again, they are not games, but they are a good precursor for spectator behavior. As they reach six months of age, babies may watch you intently throughout the song. As a part of their new interest in the external world and of their increasing interest in you they may follow your singing quite devoutly with their eyes and then, if you are very lucky, toward the end of this period they may even participate. Their sounds have now moved more to the front of the mouth and have a higher pitch. Sometimes while you are singing, they produce some of these sounds, and you sense that they are joining in. Like the dancing mentioned earlier, these sounds are quite slight, but they may be reckoned the earliest form of choir singing.

Social Games

We come now to the great *social* games of this age period. By five and six months babies are sufficiently social people that they get annoyed when you put them to bed. They even cry with rage. They know their mothers or closest caretakers and are more friendly and relaxed with them than with strangers. By the end of this age period we can say that their social world is well established. They gaze at people appropriately. They play games with their friends, and they distinguish friends from strangers.

One game that nearly every set of parents has played with their babies at some time is "This Little Pig." What this game does is to institutionalize the innumerable ways in which *anticipation* by the baby has become the name of the game of having fun. There are several ways of inducing crescendoes in order to produce fun and laughter in babies. You kiss them on the hand, on the wrist, on the elbow, on the arm, and finally on the cheek to the accompaniment of chuckles and laughter. In "This Little Pig" you tweak each little toe or finger in turn, while the old rhyme is chanted:

> This little pig went to market
> This little pig stayed home
> This little pig had roast beef [or
>   Kentucky fried chicken]
> This little pig had none.
> This little pig went wee, wee, wee,
> All the way home.

At "wee wee wee" the tickling fingers run up the child's arm or leg, terminating with a big tickle under the chin or on the stomach. There is an enuretic connotation in the adult's fun here, not that the infant knows much about that.

Another game along similar lines, using the baby's hand, is "There Was a Little Mouse." Open the baby's hand and with your forefinger make circles in her palm while you say the words to the rhyme:

> There was a little mouse,
> And he had a little house,
> And he lived—
> Up—
> Here!

At "here!" your hand travels up her arm and tickles her under her chin or arm. You can spin out the suspense in "up—here!" by lengthening the words and raising the tone of your voice. This is good for waiting rooms and the like, because you do not need props or bare feet, and although she gurgles and laughs, she does not get too hysterical.

In "Pat-a-Cake" you take hold of the baby's hands and, singing the rhyme, you pat his hands together. What is important is the keeping of rhythm in time with the rhyme. If there is any game here, it is often that the baby takes a delight in pulling his hands away, while you put them together. One set of words is:

> Pat-a-cake, pat-a-cake, baker's man,
> Bake me a cake as fast as you can.

When this rhyme was first introduced in Friedrich Fröbel's book called *Mother's Songs, Games and Rhymes*, the illustration showed the mother taking her baby into the bakery to see the baker at work, which is hardly likely to apply today. The more familiar version of the rhyme follows:

> Pat-a-cake, pat-a-cake, baker's man,
> Bake me a cake as fast as you can.
> Prick it and pat it and mark it with E,
> And put it in the oven for Emily and me!

The rhyme says "mark it with B, and put it in the oven for *baby* and me," but it is nicer to use your baby's name if it fits the rhyme. At "baby" (or "Emily") release the baby's hands and gently poke him in the stomach.

What happens after a few repetitions is that babies come to anticipate this last piece of drama and show excitement and laughter on the way to it. But not until about the end of the first year will they be playing this with you, independently clapping their own hands in time with yours.

You might as well enjoy the fact that babies are for eating and that this is what this rhyme is probably all about, hopefully all unbeknown to the baby. Perhaps the word "eating" is too specific. Parents sometimes feel they would like to "hug their babies to death," to assimilate them because they are so pleasurable. Old rhymes of this sort do not always mean just what they appear to represent. They may speak to the more complex feelings of the parents.

In "Rock-a-Bye Baby" the baby is rocked from side to side and then finally dropped and caught again. The side to side swinging leads up to the end effect. We know this is about the age, four to six months, when babies appreciate that they are creating some effect outside of themselves; for example, listening to the sounds they make as they scratch the sides of their cribs. In this game we have a much more powerful illustration of the relationship of one behavior leading to another—that is, of putting behavior together in chains.

> Rock-a-bye baby, on the tree top,
> When the wind blows, the cradle will rock.
> When the bough breaks, the cradle will fall
> And down will come baby, cradle, and all.

Clearly the baby knows nothing of the mumbo jumbo of babies and cradles and the wind in the trees nor of mothers who might sometimes fear that their babies would be dropped (and occasionally wish they could be), but both parties know they have a tiger by the tail, insofar as there is excitement to come once the series gets started.

Perhaps here, for the purists, we should say that this item and the previous one are more minor dramas than games. There is no opposition here, only a plot and an expected sequence. They share with games the importance of excitement. At this age they are probably more exciting than games can afford to be, because games have more uncertainty in them (for example, will she bite my finger or not?). The familiarity of the parent and the repetitive nature of the plot are, in a sense, the guarantee of the baby's security. They both share the same outcome.

THE BABY'S OWN PLAY

It is not as hard for babies to handle their food now, so they engage in *food play*. They "play" with their cereal with relaxed manipulation of it by mouths and hands. They spurt the cereal out of their mouths, showing some satisfaction in seeing it spatter all over. They can be obstinate in spitting out the food you are spooning into them. Most mothers keep their babies' hands out of the way while feeding them, but if they are left to themselves, their hands, fingers, and blowing all mix together, and you can tell from the smiles on their faces that this is the "pleasurable digressive activity" that we call play.

When the urgent phases of feeding are over, *nipple play* begins. Babies play with the nipple, using their fingers and thumbs in opposition, pinching it in either hand. They also push the nipple in and out of their mouths with strong little tongues. They put the nipple on one side of their mouths and chew on it. Although breast feeding may be favored for other reasons, it is fairly obvious that a rubber nipple on a bottle is more fun for babies to play with.

Babies smile at familiar faces a lot now. The enjoyment of looking at familiar faces is, for a time, almost a form of play, as if they are enjoying looking at things well known and perhaps seeing if they can see something different about the dearly familiar faces. They are certainly quick to spy earrings on their mothers and just as quick to pull them off.

A great deal of time is also spent staring and smiling at familiar objects. A jar of flowers or the animals on the crib border might seem to be old friends. The role of just looking and looking has probably been underestimated. Just as friendly faces are distinguished from strange faces, so do other faces, such as those of dolls, become more exciting. There is a place for dolls, which are all head for the six-month-old. Do not worry about bodies. They do not know those yet. A series of heads with different kinds of faces, shapes, and sizes of noses, ears, eyes, and mouths is what is called for in this period. They should also be suckable of course. We could also make quite a case for *hand* toys. What fascinates three- to six-month-olds are their own hands, but we will return to that later, because their own hands are, in a sense, always the most available toy. All of this looking enjoyment might be called *recognition play*.

Such play is like *spectator play*. This is hard to understand but is noticeable in babies who have mobiles that they have grown accustomed to and that move. There are clearly times when babies seem completely aroused by the movements. For example, some parents may want to cut a small shape like a hand out of cardboard. Babies have spent so much time looking at their own hands over the prior four months that this seems a most appropriate object to look at. Watching it move can cause babies little spasms of excitement and cries that seem almost to indicate an intoxication of interest. They open their eyes wide and may open and close them as the hand swings with crib movement or air currents. The nearest equivalent to such excitement in adulthood seems to be spectator sports.

Babies are more comfortable with the things they know well. They are less tense or stiff. They breathe regularly, their pulse rates are normal, their faces do not appear flushed, and they babble normally. When these signs of relaxation are present, we may assume that their dabbling with objects in and out of their mouths and hands is a play for variability that is within their easy control. This is *object play*.

Their main toy is their *hand*. They play with different fingers, pushing them in and out of their mouths, chomping on them, pulling them out, babbling with them endlessly. Occasionally, they almost choke themselves. Sometimes, the constant weaving, twisting, and intertwining of their fingers and hands in front of their faces have an almost balletlike character. It is like the endless ruminative mouth play of the first three months. Their hands have taken their mouths' place as the major ruminator. They also like to examine *your* hand, hold it in front of their heads, and move it slowly toward them. A hand mobile would be as effective now as a nipple mobile would be earlier.

They get wildly excited when their own movements cause their mobile to move or when they pull at their cradle gym and get everything ringing. Apparently they are becoming aware (four months plus) that *they* are causing things to happen. This is *causal play*. Their mobile swings around wildly as a result of their pulling it. They open and shut their eyes in surprise and delight. They get more and more ecstatic. These self-initiated jags are about as exciting as making them laugh. This is fiesta time in their miniworld, if wild excitement and delight can be so described.

To sum it up, by six months we have had the following peaks of excitement: feeding in months one and two, eye-love in months two to four, laughter in months three to five, and making things happen in months four to six.

4 | Joining Society:

From Six to Twelve Months

She had a passion for being held hanging by her ankles and looking at the world from upside down.

•

He loved to be held and to flap his legs alternately as if walking.

•

She loved to stick her fingers up my nose.

In the second half of the first year many important things happen in babies' play life. The most important is that they begin to be able to take the initiative in many of the games we play with them. They actually start the games themselves. These games have a more *social* give-and-take quality. In their own play babies are also much more active. During this period they sit up, stand, and begin to walk. They begin to get into everything. Their own actions take on much more meaning than we could see before, partly because their own play is that much easier to recognize. Play in the first six months has been so fleeting that we could not always say as much about it as we would like.

By this age children also can do some of their own communicating. They may have a word to say, perhaps "Mama." At least they respond to their name and sometimes a command or two, such as "stop." Actually they are responding to the feel of these things, taking in your facial and arm expressions at the same time as the word, so that responding to the words associated with them correctly is no mystery. There is much imitation of gesture—waving bye-bye, shrugging, following a pointed hand. The melody of our communications is there in these six months even before the full meaning.

So what with their starting the games we have already played with them, imitating us, and being in touch with our expressions, they, as our partners, have become real game players.

GAMES AND OTHER THINGS TO DO

Finger Sucking

At six to seven months babies begin to sit up. This seems to put them in contact with people and things. They reach out, even lunge for objects. They enjoy pushing, pulling, and twisting any gadgets, knobs, or toys that are within reach or banging with anything they can hold. They discover the rest of their bodies. They even suck their toes, something we would like to be agile enough to do in later years. Finger sucking is an oral game that still works. You suck their fingers into your mouth, and they pull them out. They have been sucking your fingers for months and now are fascinated by your doing the opposite. We should warn you that sticking their fingers up your nose or in your eyes is a side play that they will enjoy if they get the chance.

Mock Falling

With mock falling you stand the baby on your lap, hold his hands, and then let him fall. With a great cry he falls backward, only to be held firmly by the hands. If you do this right, with the proper anticipation and balking, this is really exciting for him. There are innumerable variations of this that you can invent. At this age, for example, some infants are crazy about hanging upside down or being dropped and caught. These minor forms of vertigo are presumably the beginnings of the circus and carnival impulses. Here we first manifest our delight for those forms of disorientation that are later packaged into roller coasters, tightwire performances, and merry-go-rounds. Some sturdy children even enjoy being thrown from person to person like a football. We would not advise it for most. Passing is fun enough.

Bed Roughhousing

Your bed is always a great place for babies. They can hide under the blankets when they are in bed with your knees holding the blankets up. Then they come crawling out. They can slide down the slide of your legs. They can be sat on your knees and suddenly plopped down as the knees go flat. But those are all games that leave you in the bed. Bed roughhousing is using the bed as a trampoline, as we did in the last chapter. Now, however, we add the crescendo of numbers—"one, two, three, and *up*"—thus adding anticipation to the mayhem. The same "one, two, three, and up" principle can be used by two parents swinging their child when out for a walk. On "up" they lift the baby into the air as they walk along. Babies will play this one until either your arms or theirs fall off.

The Game of Give and Take

The big new games of this age are *social* rather than physical. You give something to them, and then you take it away. It can be a book or a toy or a newspaper. After a few repetitions they grab it back. Then later they give it to you and take it back. In a short time you are both grabbing it from each other. This is the beginning of the great market game. They are doing the same thing when they share their wet cookie with you. One suck for them, one for you.

Although it sounds very simple, a great deal of social growth has been necessary for this to happen. Babies can now interpret many of your expressions (of happiness, anger, scolding), and you can interpret theirs. You know the meaning of their different cries. There are different cries for hunger, pain, and annoyance. This insight into how each other is feeling is an important part of social games like this. Let us say again though that, as with all other games, it is "staged" by you. Your mock surprise and annoyance when they take the object away are the important elements that account for the baby's merriment.

It is usually not until the end of the first year that babies will "give" things to people in order to enjoy their pleasurable response—the "thank you" and "how nice." Usually they want them back immediately, so they can play the game with someone else. This is not the last time we will find a social relationship occurring in a game before it occurs in ordinary relationships. That is, the give and take is experienced in game play before children can manage it or understand it themselves in ordinary social activity.

Peek-a-Boo

Peek-a-boo does not have to be with a person to begin with, although that is the most usual way to catch infants' attention. When you and they have been playing with a toy, if you suddenly make it disappear and then reappear, this can lead first to surprise, then to delight, and then to peals of laughter after several repetitions. In person, you play the game by popping up beside their crib after disappearing or you pop up from behind the table. It is a very special thing to watch babies anticipating the emergence of their mothers' or fathers' heads, with their mouths and eyes wide open. As the head pops into view, they often show a slightly startled effect, and then their faces burst into broad smiles. It will be some months yet before the babies themselves look for things that are lost. But as early as seven or eight months you can produce these startle and amusement effects by making things or yourself reappear quickly.

We know that in this second year of life babies are sometimes upset by strangers. What we parents seem to do in this game is momentarily make ourselves into strangers. But our suddenly popping up head, momentarily taken for something else, is quickly recognized, and the aroused anxiety collapses into enjoyment. Children made versatile by such play might more easily handle the onset of strangers, although we are aware of no research on that possibility as yet.

Bury the Baby

In the game of bury the baby you throw the baby's own light comfort blanket over her head, then pull it off. As with other games the introduction must be accompanied with smiles, so that the baby is relaxed and reassured. At first the baby is a little startled but is then pleased to see your face again. She then anticipates the blanket, pulls it off by herself, and the game has begun in earnest. You cover her, she uncovers herself, you cover, she uncovers.

Hear-a-Boo

Hear-a-boo is the same as peek-a-boo, but now you are making a noise with a bell, and he is looking for it as you slide your hand behind him, underneath his chair, etc. You do not hide your hand so much as put it out of his line of vision; then he has to switch his head somewhere else to be able to see it.

Crackle

Crumple a sheet of newspaper so it makes a lot of noise and throw it onto the baby's head and face, showering down on her. First make the big crackling noise until she is enjoying that, then throw it at her head. You can repeat this until she is deep in a pile of newspaper and she flails around enjoying herself.

Chase the Dog

If you have a nice old dog that runs away from little babies, infants love to be carried around chasing the dog. They cannot run after the dog by themselves yet. Needless to say, six-month-old babies are enraptured by dogs and will bury their faces and mouths in their hair and suck it. Whether you want that for your dog or for your baby is something else.

Ride the Camel

The camel is one of the parents sitting on the floor with hands behind his or her back and legs bent. You walk on feet and hands, tummy up. As you move along like a four-legged animal, you get a weaving, bobbing camel effect. This is a safer mode of transport at this age than carrying children on your back because they can be cradled on your stomach and you can sink quickly to the floor if they seem about to flip off.

Riding on your back does not come until some time during the second year, and even then it is sometimes hard to hold the baby on. Often you find yourself giving your eighteen-month-old a horsey ride on your back with one hand high up behind you trying to stump along on all fours, only it is all threes. Usually this is not good for very much transport. Your arms cannot take it, but the baby is happy to sit and wait on your back as you lie on your face waiting to recover.

Funny Faces

Making funny faces is one of the great games for the last few months of the first year. From about six months onward children usually begin to get more or less apprehensive about the faces of strangers. As they become more settled with the familiar people in their own home, they become more intrigued by the faces of strangers. The differences in these other faces fascinate them and sometimes scare them. We have seen children at this age become upset by the face on a toy if it was strange enough. A game that this stage permits is the making of funny faces by familiar people. Babies now love your most clownlike and weirdest faces.

You can make things more dramatic by galloping up to the sitting baby on all fours wearing such a funny face. Another variety is to make a funny face when they pull off your dark glasses, which infants love to do when they get the chance.

Mirror Faces

You can play a game of making funny faces in the mirror for the baby to see. Babies recognize themselves in the mirror in some sense and they recognize you too. At least there is research evidence that babies are not as disturbed by seeing themselves in the mirror as they are by seeing strangers. Thus, looking at each other in the mirror and then back to each other's faces, with some funny faces thrown in, is an amusing pastime.

Book Peek-a-Boo

If you have a simple picture book of animals, you can make an animal sound to match each picture. Then try quickly opening the book and making the sound of the picture you find. Keep opening and closing the book. This is combining peek-a-boo with a contest of showing the animal and shutting the book while the baby tries to hold it, or you try to hold the picture while the baby tries to turn the page or throw the book away. Do not use books that are heirlooms.

By twelve months children sometimes will turn pages on their own and babble expressively as if they are reading. They are imitating your reading to them. This roughhouse with books and the baby's own page turning and reading will not occur unless you have been telling stories to them with picture books or, rather, acting out the animal noises. Although this can all occur by twelve months, it is more typical of the second year, when the baby has had more outings and has seen more animals.

Laughing

By now there are many ways of making babies laugh. All the methods of play mentioned in the first six months will probably work better now. When we play with children in the early months, laughter is a major achievement. Now it is easy and is a natural outcome of almost every game we have described. By and large, the noise-making and touching forms of laughter making are better in the earlier months (six to eight months), and the social and visual forms become better later (nine to twelve months).

Funny noises—sounds in an unusual sequence, with the last part different, taking longer, or whatever—and high-pitched funny voices are good laugh makers during the first year but seem to become less effective toward the end of the year.

Bouncing babies, suspending them, blowing on their faces, kissing their stomachs, stroking their cheeks, tickling them under the chin, and blowing raspberries on their necks are better in about midyear, six to nine months.

Socially produced laughter—which you get from "This Little Pig," rushing up to babies and grabbing them with anticipatory cries, throwing the blanket over their faces, etc.—is more successful as the year goes by.

Visually produced laughter also improves throughout the year, such as your walking in a funny way, falling over and making a spectacle of yourself, or two parents' jumping about and making an object disappear and reappear.

THE BABY'S OWN PLAY

When we move to what children are doing as compared with what we have been doing with children, the focus must be more on *action* and less on these amusing social events. Furthermore, these actions comprise the bulk of their play. Our social games are usually just a small part of their total play time.

Exploratory Actions with Basic Forces

The big difference is that babies can crawl at around seven to nine months of age and pull themselves up to stand and sometimes walk at about ten to eleven months. They are now as interested in what they can do as in what we have to show them. A sense of themselves as the ones who do things is dawning. You are beginning to be ever so slightly phased out.

They go about sticking a stiff little finger into every crevice. They are fascinated by teeny weeny crumbs on the floor or old cereal pieces under the sofa. They test everything with their mouths—sand, dirt, bits of fluff. They are fascinated by all small objects and knobs and explore the world of cupboard handles and TV switches. It is surprising how many things there are around that are like nipples and, as such, seem good to chew. Obviously you have to think about what is lying around that is dirty or dangerous or precious, because such things can be hazards for the locomoting explorer.

By eleven and twelve months they are all over the floor, either crawling or taking steps between the sofas or moving around the sides of the furniture, holding on. (Some toy designer should dream up some maze equipment for nine- to eighteen-month-olds; it could be patterned after a maze with toys hanging at various intervals, the whole thing about two feet high, for babies to make their way through. Although it would be a cumbersome toy, if it were ingeniously designed, it would be useful for some good explorations. But where would you put it? It would have to be able to be put away or it could become as limiting as a playpen can be.)

The actions babies can now carry out are almost endless. We are only going to list the main ones. What we want to emphasize is that they must learn these actions by trying them out. It is as if they were learning to use their hands, arms, and bodies as *forces* that they could apply to the world.

Judging by the amount of time they spend at it, during the second half of the first year infants are very concerned about mastering such forces as *banging, inserting* (poking) small objects into spaces, *twisting* or turning knobs, *pushing* and *pulling* movable objects, crawling *under* things (such as tables and chairs), getting *into* things (such as cupboards under the sink), *opening* and *shutting* doors, pulling drawers *in and out*, getting in and out of cardboard boxes, *climbing* stairs, *squeezing* water out of sponges, and *dropping* objects from heights.

These forces, when they are mastered, become the basis for

the children's playfulness. Thus, banging things that are held in the hand, which is carefully mastered first, later becomes one of the earliest forces to lead to hilarious enjoyment with the noises that they make. They delight in banging toys, newspapers, and the like on the table. Such variety, when it is added to previous mastery, is the height of playfulness. That babies can also get your attention and, if they are lucky, a smile, probably makes it that much more rewarding.

The approval babies get from their parents for all their feats is a very important part of the baby-parent relationship. In many of the games described in the first six months the fun for the infants is that they are the audience anticipating the adults' making things happen. Now the coin is turned, and we have some dramatic displays by them, although we might say that these are generally all climax, with little opportunity yet for plotted anticipation. Making a loud banging noise with a spoon is the whole drama. Anticipation will come during the next year, when the child, yelling peek-a-boo from far off, comes running around the corner of the kitchen door. At this age, six to twelve months, the baby's exultation at making a big noise is the performance itself.

Any of the new-found skills can become the basis for fun. The psychologist Jean Piaget in his book *Play, Dreams and Imitation in Childhood* (Norton) gives the example of his ten-month-old daughter who, putting her nose close to her mother's cheek, discovered that she was forced to breath harder. This interested her and, presumably because she was already a master at blowing against obstacles, she did not just repeat the process; she immediately complicated it for the fun of it. She drew back an inch or so, screwed up her nose, sniffed and breathed out alternately very hard (as if blowing her nose), and then again thrust her nose against her mother's cheek, laughing heartily. These actions went on every day for quite some time and were a kind of ritual game of child with mother's cheek.

New Ideas for Appropriate Toys

If the discovery of basic forces and their control is as important as we have suggested here, it also follows that the right kinds of toys and objects ought to be critical for young children—objects to suck and bang or to climb into, things made of toweling, wood, or plastic (not the kind that breaks easily), and cardboard boxes.

We have already suggested a few toy inventions in previous chapters. Let us "play" with a few more for the creative parent who knows how to engineer objects. For the first six months we have had face dolls and hand dolls; some additional ideas follow for those months. A *mobile* should be simple, and it should be able to move as a result of the baby's movement or wriggling in the crib.

The parent might wear a variety of kinds of *necklaces* for the baby to grasp, suck, and tinker with. For example, you can thread large wooden beads, or even empty spools that you have colored yourself, on to elastic to make a necklace. The baby can pull and explore the different shapes. You can also tie lengths of different-colored cord or braid together. You can attach small articles of different textures to hang from these, such as keys, bells, and furry balls. Naturally, it is better to wear one necklace for a while and then substitute one that is slightly different. The difference leads to surprise and to examination. Babies are fascinated by any jewelry that a mother wears anyway, so they might as well have some childproof jewelry to play with while they are drinking their bottles.

A *pacifier* might have several nipples of different sizes and softness. It would be an education for the mouth. It must be safe to suck and impossible to swallow, and it must not hurt if accidentally banged against the baby's face. A *tracker* could be an apparatus on the crib that would release an object that goes from side to side across the top of the crib when the infant pulls a suspended cord. Each tug would put it in motion, and babies would be able to track it with their eyes (good for future bird watchers). A *grasper* would be a device for grasping. It would have holes for your fingers to go into. There would be one-finger, two-finger, and three-finger holes. When squeezed at one end, all the weight could move to the other end.

Toys for the second six months can be more complex. Good ones illustrate the principle that what babies do with the toy must produce some other effect. The good old-fashioned *jack-in-the-box* nicely illustrates the effect of doing one thing (winding it up) and getting another action (the Jack popping up). That toy can be appropriate at the end of the first year, although more so during the second, since it also includes a strange face and a sudden startling action, which the baby must get used to. The tune that goes with winding it up gets the baby ready for it.

What is interesting about toys appropriate for the second half of the first year is that they lead beyond the children's major line of activity. Babies are largely growing used to their own application of power and what they can control. These toys work on the edge of their dawning consciousness of the effects created by different forms of their power. *Nesting boxes*, which are so popular at this time as a way of putting things into things and taking them out again, can be made more sophisticated by being transparent and permitting babies to see animal pictures when they get them together in a certain way. Another possibility might be a flashlight, attached to the crib, that works to produce changing *shadow patterns* on the white end of the crib as the baby pushes buttons on it.

We suggest toys like this to illustrate the basic idea that what babies do with the toy must produce some other effect. In the *bing-bonger*, for example, when the babies turn the toy upside down, a metal ball bearing inside runs down to one end and produces a tone; when the toy is turned up the other way, the ball bearing runs down to the other end and produces a different tone. Each end is differently colored. This way the babies can produce an immediate effect, but they also produce a puzzle for themselves. Why the different sounds? With careful discriminating they will in due course learn to associate sound and color and be able to anticipate what sound they will get when they have the particular color on the bottom.

These have been some of our dreams. You can also have fun dreaming up toys for the toy companies to make and then testing their catalogs to see how good they are.

Adding this kind of effect to the toy enlarges its life well into the second year—that is, if you can still find the pieces, which is the handicap with all these schemes for infant toys of an intricate sort; you lose the bits. Anyway, there are always pots and pans, and they seldom get lost; or at least, if you cannot find them in the kitchen, they will be in the bath.

We assume that those who play a lot with their babies in the first year of life will have babies who continue to be playful in the following years. The shifting of position and the creation of excitement in physical actions certainly suggest themselves as the beginning for the more imaginative and intellectual versatility of the years to come. Versatility in one should lead to versatility in the other. At least that is our assumption. It seems a reasonable one to us.

5 | Mastery is Not Play:

From One to Two Years

He is peep-ohing from everywhere, under the coffee table, through the banisters, and round the corner. Each time we are supposed to light up with surprise and joy and cry "There he is!"

•

She made a big face when she tasted my coffee. We all laughed. After that, whenever we have coffee, she makes a big face and expects us to laugh.

•

They like to be thrown high into the air and caught again.

•

He climbs on the kitchen table and mixes the butter in his hair and the coffee all over his face. He dips his fingers in the sugar. Whenever we hear a chair scraping along the kitchen floor, we know he is heading for that breakfast.

•

She gives a big smile and says "Hi" whenever she sees you, all day long, a hundred times a day.

•

He pushes his bottle into the Teddy's mouth and says "all gone."

•

She climbs on her father's back and cries "Ride the horse."

As infants' activities get more complex, we have to decide what is play and what is not. It was hard to make this distinction earlier, but now perhaps we can. First there are the games they play with us. We will call those play. Then toward the end of the second year they begin to pretend things. They start make-believe. Now everyone accepts that this is a type of play. Adults just do not go around pretending to play house, but children do, so that must be play. But when we get beyond that into all their other activities, it is often hard to know what they are. Later in this chapter we want to introduce a distinction between activities children carry out to learn or to master things and activities they carry out for play.

But first, before we get into games, there are a few important things to be said about what infants are like in this second year. Some authorities hold that it is between about ten months and eighteen months that babies are most affected by what you do to them. They argue that, until then, babies just are not social enough to be much influenced by you (unless you neglect them terribly).

But at this age period, because they can walk about and get into everything, you begin to show your approval and disapproval more clearly. You either let them have a lot of freedom to move about and get into everything or else you restrict them a great deal because of the nuisance they are or the danger they may get into, or you do something in between. But whatever you do, it begins to set the pattern for how much free behavior babies learn to take for granted.

Again at this age they are beginning to say their first few words. You either encourage this by talking with them a lot or you do not. So you have a talker on your hands or you have a quiet one. Finally, toward the end of the second year babies begin to get a sense of who they are. They begin to realize that they can make decisions, and so they do not like to be bossed about quite as much. They often begin to show a stubborn unwillingness to do everything you expect. Having discovered that they can make choices, they often act as if only *they* can make a choice.

How you handle this negativism, how you make it possible for both of you to make choices, makes a big difference. When our eldest daughter was about thirteen months old, she discovered that if someone said "please" to her and then she did what they asked ("get the paper please," "please get out of the way"), everyone rewarded her tremendously and said how wonderful she was. As long as we said "please," she would do whatever we wanted. But it increasingly became a form of slavery for her. One day when she was about two years old, she finally revolted in the only way she knew how. "Don't say please!" she cried. She was winning her freedom to choose for herself, regardless of the sweetness of our request.

The major issues then between parent and child are mobility, language, and choice. In addition to these we can describe children during this year as follows. They begin by walking and end by running. They climb stairs and tables and everything else. They get into cupboards and under beds and into toilets. They love stuffing towels down toilets. They push chairs to tables and climb up and play with the remnants of breakfast. They are not able to distinguish a Ming vase from an old lamp stand and will grab hold of or push either with the same concern for action and unconcern for auction. They like to feed and dress themselves and do both with difficulty and mess. They begin to scribble.

They are also beginning to be thinkers and may by the end of this year know what you mean when you use some numbers (one and many), a color or two (red), a size (big and small), or some animals (dog, cat) and may like to organize their toys in different piles. They chatter at the table when you chatter. They have a number of words they use expressively, such as "Hi," "more," "doggie," and "Mama." From now on games with your baby are going to have more complexity.

GAMES AND OTHER THINGS TO DO

Chasing

The game of chasing keeps appearing on these pages. This is partly because it is in some senses the major game of mankind. There are more varieties of chasing than anything else. As soon as babies can walk with some skill, they can begin to chase you. Just as you had them chase the dog *with* you before, now they will strut after you as you hobble away on all fours. We assume that you will be down on the floor with them. There is not much sense to this game otherwise. You gallop behind the sofa or behind the chairs, and they come shrieking after you. Then when you turn and grab them, both of you roll on the floor with laughter.

At this time babies are still only chasers. They have not learned to run away yet. This is an important point. It seems to show that when we learn to behave socially, we first learn just one side of the relationship. Later we learn the other side. Then still later we put them both together. So here children learn the social relationship of chasing and escaping, first by chasing, next by escaping, then with both together.

By eighteen months the babies who have chased you on all your fours the last six months will now seek to have you chase them. You will chase them around the sofa or up the stairs. They favor being chased up the stairs, preceded by peeping through the bannisters. Here the old game, the chase, is applied to the new motor difficulty, getting up the stairs quickly. Chasing by babies is now more interesting also. It can cover several rooms and be accompanied by cries and signals from you. Note that in neither of these do we yet have role switching in the same game. You either chase or are chased—one game at a time.

These games of chasing go on almost universally, and although many other things have changed, children today still play this game almost as frequently as they used to. In addition, it seems to be related to a very basic human conflict over how we feel about other people, whether to *approach* them or to *avoid* them. We have seen that in the first year of life babies learned to tell the difference between their close caretakers and other people and then began to show either some apprehension or relative indifference toward others.

Many psychologists have written about this fear of strangers, which seems to peak at the end of the first year. Its extent appears to depend partly on how many elders looked after the baby in the first place. Babies brought up in a rather solitary way by one person seem more likely to show this fear than do babies who have had many people care for them. One of our babies showed this apprehension only by smiling more at us (than she usually did) when strangers were around! Anyway, the apprehension is there. One never knows for sure what the stranger will do. Does he bring reward or punishment?

Hide the Thimble

Another thing babies know by about ten months is that out of sight is not out of mind. Up until then babies have not generally known how to search for things that have disappeared. At this time they begin to show preliminary search capacities, so that if you show them a bright toy and then hide it under your hand, they will pull your hand away. Hide the toy, or doll, or book, or slipper, or in the old days the thimble is based on that interest.

When you sit with the baby on your lap or beside you, there are innumerable ways you can show an object and then cover it. The younger the baby, the more of the object he must be able to see. As children move into the second year, however, they will learn to look all over, rather than just under the obvious place where they have seen you hide it, although at this age they are pretty much limited to that. Once again cries of excitement as the object is revealed are in order.

Peeping

We make much of peep-oh these days in psychology because it tells us that children still remember objects when they cannot see them, a knowledge that dawns about the end of the first year. Before that time, if they cannot see an object, they forget it. Even putting their bottles out of sight decreases their hunger a little. Peeping is like chasing in being one of the major games of mankind. There are many games in which peeping or spying is combined with chasing, such as hide and seek.

Babies now begin to play peeping from anywhere. They peep out at you from under the table, from under chairs, from under the blankets on the bed. Sometimes it is casual. Sometimes it is a waiting game, in which their heads suddenly pop out. They often burst into laughter before they can even say "peep-oh." There is an interesting reversal here, insofar as you are now the one who is "peeped" at, just as the baby was during the previous six months. We quite often react to peeping by chasing the peeper, so that the two play activities easily get linked together.

Audience Games

The one-sidedness of the previous behavior takes us naturally to all those times that, as a parent, your main function seems to be to provide the enjoying audience. For example, one form of peeping is for the baby to come running out from behind the door and for you to pretend to look all surprised. This is, in a way, an early form of coming "on stage." We might call it a game of entrances (perhaps chasing is a game of exits). Babies are often "on stage" during this year. In fact, almost any time you laugh or enjoy anything, it is likely to be repeated. The baby who is given a little coffee and makes a grimace that draws laughter will, the next time she sees the coffee, put on the same face and then look for the laughter.

Clearly we can say that while in the first year we taught the baby the elements of theater, the drama of anticipation and crescendo, this year we are teaching exits, entrances, and on-stage performances. Oddly enough, audience behavior gets mimicked too. By midyear babies can build a small tower of a few blocks. They build it. They knock it down. We clap. They clap. They may not have distinguished yet who claps for whom, but they do know to clap when others are clapping. It is Russian clapping!

Losing People

Losing people is a pretend game in that someone who is sitting right next to you is lost. You and the baby go about saying "Where's Mommy?" and look everywhere, behind her, underneath, and so forth, and then finally yell with great surprise, "Oh, here she is!" The baby usually cannot abide the delay and beats you to the punch, crying "Here she is!"

Hugging

With great éclat you and the baby hug each other in turns. A hugging exhibition also may be a pretense meeting: "Oh hullo, I haven't seen you for years." Note that this principle of alternating responses, or taking turns, which you have been using since the earliest games, will become the major piece of equipment for the child in later social play.

Horseplay

Horseplay activities have enlarged in scope. Children who have been built up for it since babies are now swung high in the air by their parents, thrown up and caught (preferably above the bed). They can be swung around by the ankles or by the wrists. These games, as well as tricycle pushing (which they demand) and riding on various contraptions at a country fair, all come under the heading of *vertigo*, the power one gets from feeling safe when in fact one no longer has body control. Given that so much of these early years are devoted to the gaining of such body control, these enjoyments seem natural enough.

Emptying

You put the toys back in the box, they throw them out. It is a hilarious race to see who can achieve the end of emptying or filling first. It seems to work better as emptying than as filling, although the latter has a better moral principle going for it.

Catching

A simple game of catching is not easily maintained, but if the baby sits against a wall, legs apart, and you roll the ball, that can help; or you can throw something like a comb to each other at opposite ends of the sofa. The distinction between catching and throwing is not too clear in this game, but the idea of an alternating exchange is present.

Hard Heads and Other Hard Parts

For those who can take it, banging heads together gently is a game that some enjoy. There are innumerable games to be invented with bodies. There are parent hand spiders that tickle and crawl up the baby's legs until he sits on them. There are legs that keep falling on top of the baby, who struggles out from under. Likewise, you can lie on the floor and allow yourself to be walked on or jumped on. This is usually part of being ridden as a horse or ridden as a rocking boat. (Can the baby stay on while you rock? Can *all* your children stay on as you rock and roll your body-boat on the floor? It is a very hard game after dinner!)

Games of Retrieval

This is the game you play with your dog, known as "Fido Fetch the Bone." Children are at about that play level at this age and will find great excitement in the back and forward fetching of something. The game can be varied by having them take the object (ball, doll, etc.) to other, named people in the room. Although they may not be able to say the names of their brothers or sisters or relatives, they can often recognize them when they are named and bring them the object.

Mock Disapproval

Mock disapproval involves pretended outrage at an offense, as when the baby knocks down a tower of blocks you have built. Then you seize her and pretend to scold her. But she knocks them down again, and you get angry again, and so forth. The mock scolding means seizing and roughing up (gently) and yelling and spanking, all with fiery zeal and with a crazily distorted face and voice. Here, as elsewhere, the manner of the theatrics and the clowning provides the guarantee that this is a play frame, not a real one.

Phony Birthdays

Wrap up his toys in paper and tie them lightly with string. "Here's a present." But he should see the whole process, since this is a game of unwrapping, not an economical way of getting through Christmas. Mock exaggeration of gift giving is in order, as is the singing of "Happy Birthday" with pretended surprise and pleasure at the gift.

Tug-of-War

Tie two pieces of string to a pull toy or to a strong cart. Then both of you pull at it from different directions. Alternate pulling hard with easing up. Remember, you are not supposed to win, just to provide the tension of mild contest.

"Here Is a Beehive"

"Here Is a Beehive" is a finger game in which the hand is held as a fist and the fingers are released one at a time. Some say the following ditty:

Here is a beehive. Where are the bees?
Hidden away where nobody sees.
Soon they come, creeping out of the hive,
One, two, three, four, five.

Which Hand?

In this game you hide an object in one hand or the other, and the child has to find out which one. These games begin with fairly obvious indications by you of the hand that holds the coin or block. But as the year proceeds, increasing amounts of deceptive hanky-panky can be added. The child always gets it on the second guess anyway. The same game can be played hiding the object under inverted cups.

There are many finger and hand games that babies love at this age. Some we perform on them; for example,

Knock at the door, [knock on their forehead]
Ring the bell, [tug gently at their hair]
Peep in, [open their eye]
Lift the latch, [tweak their nose up]
And *walk in*! [pop your finger in their mouth]

Also, gently tap each of their finger tips, beginning with the little one, and say

Hey Johnny, Johnny, Johnny, Johnny,
Whoops [slide your finger down the slide of their
      forefinger and land on their thumb] Johnny,
      whoops [slide back up again]
Johnny, [and tap all the fingers again] Johnny,
      Johnny, Johnny. [or "Emmy, Emmy, Emmy"]

Other such games babies watch you perform, such as
"Here's the Church, and Here's the Steeple" or "Eency
Weency Spider." You can also take all the jump-rope rhymes
or counting-out rhymes that you remember and "count out"
the buttons on their sweaters or their ears, eyes, noses, etc.
The simple, funny-sounding ones work best:

> Inky, pinky, ponky, Daddy bought a donkey,
> Donkey died, Daddy cried, Inky, pinky, ponky.

A Commentary on These Games with Parents

One has to be impressed that these games are more complex than anything else these children can do socially at this
age. Where else will we see chasing and being chased, search-
ing for toys you have hidden, peeping and running, throwing
and retrieving, making on-stage entrances, making faces for
an audience, making exits (running from the room), clapping as an audience does, and pretending to lose someone, to
greet someone, to offend and to be scolded, and to unwrap
gifts.

Babies do not carry out social performances that are this
complex outside of the games they play. Of course, it is your
support that helps them to play a part in these games. But
perhaps even more important than that, a game can deal with
social relations like this because it does not have to deal with
anything else. Thus, you can play chasing and being chased
easily, because you do not also have to worry about being
mother and baby or getting the dinner or whether the infant
will be hurt or will fall over. You have chosen a safe place.
You have the time to do it. Both you and the baby know that
it is for fun, which also means that nothing will happen that
you have not expected to happen. Everything is manageable.
You both have control of the situation, and although there is

to be the excitement of the chase, there is nothing else (barring accidents) that you have to worry about.

All play has these characteristics. You have to be *relaxed* and let your excitements occur only in ways that allow you to continue to feel safe about them. There is always this background feeling of being at your ease. You have to feel that you are in *control* of events, rather than events' controlling you. You can do this because the play or the game is not the total complexity of life. It is just a selected part of life, like chasing—which is to say that it is an *abstract* or a blueprint of one part of reality. This then is our definition of what both play and games have in common. They occur in certain conditions of player relaxation, player control, and abstraction from the world around.

Perhaps this is the truth of that old statement that play and games prepare you for life. They are not a preparation for life as it is lived in all its complexity, but they are a preparation in a simplified way. It is like learning the alphabet, which does not mean you can read, but it helps; or learning numbers, which does not mean you can do arithmetic, but it helps. Playing chasing does not mean you know how to avoid dangers, but it helps. Coming on stage and making exits do not help you to be graceful or diplomatic socially, but they make a contribution. Games give us such an alphabet of human society. They select out one piece of social behavior at a time for us to learn and to practice. In ordinary life we have to learn all these things all mixed together, and it is much more difficult. Games give us a head start on our social engagements.

THE CHILD'S OWN PLAY

But social games are just a small part of children's free activity. Most of their time goes into their own actions. Although we are giving less space to these, that does not mean they are less important to the children. It is just that they are so innumerable that we have space only to alert you to their existence. These lists, however, suggest a basis for other games you might invent. We list the activities rather than describe them.

We have divided the child's own actions into two groups: exploration and testing.

In *exploration* children want to understand the *relationships between things*. First they want to know what is there. What is under the table? What is in the cupboard? What is behind the back fence? Second they want to know what affects what. If you slam the cupboard door, will the pots fall over? If you get under the table, will you find your ball? Will you find your older brother behind the back fence?

In trying to understand the relationships between things and what causes what, children are like miniature scientists. Their explorations are the first forms of scientific activity. In later years we will find that there continue to be children who prefer this sort of analytic exploratory play, just as in adulthood there continue to be people who prefer to understand the world in scientific terms.

In *testing* children are concerned with *testing out what they can do*. It is not always easy to tell in the first year whether children are exploring the way things are or finding out what they can do with them. But as the years go by the difference becomes obvious. Climbing trees, riding bicycles, balancing on planks, pushing another child off the step are all ways of testing oneself out. You test out your body, what it can do and what it cannot do. You take a "dare" and prove you can do more than the others said you could. You test out your social skills by arguing, fighting, or being cunning. In later life you jump out of airplanes, you climb mountains, you explore the bottom of the sea, all of which require courage.

This is a form of mastery that requires you to assert yourself to predict what you can do and then to follow it up to see if you can. If you can do what you have said, then you have proven your mastery and your understanding. All the great adventurers, sailors, and "explorers" have followed this route to knowledge. And as all parents who have very active little boys or girls know, this seems to be a favored way of knowing for some children, usually for those who get the most injuries. This is the form of education that has been called "learning through doing," although the advocates of this type of learning did not always have in mind the reckless forms that some children engage in.

Exploration and Testing: Activities and Materials

The following examples of exploratory and testing activities also outline the type of toys and apparatus it is useful to have at this time for the child's growth, not that we suggest you need *all* of these.

EXAMPLES OF EXPLORATORY ACTIVITY

Activity	Objects with Which the Baby Is Often Concerned
Hammering, pounding, beating	Wooden peg board, drum, clay
Touching, fingering	Textures, shapes, edges, piano keys
Turning	Book pages
Looking, inspecting	Books, pictures

EXAMPLES OF EXPLORATORY ACTIVITY (*continued*)

Activity	Objects with Which the Baby Is Often Concerned
Emptying, filling	Sand, buckets, boxes, blocks, containers, pots
Threading	Beads, empty spools for thread
Opening, shutting	Doors, drawers
Stacking, knocking down	Blocks
Picking up	Counters
Twisting	Knobs, switches
Bouncing, rolling, retrieving	Balls, beds, armchairs
Crayoning	Newspaper, paper bags, paper
Creeping, crawling through	Boxes, barrels
Dropping	Spoons, cereal bowls

For exploration to proceed at its best the materials used need some attention. *Blocks*, for example, ought to be large and small, round, square, triangular, wide and narrow, high and low, deep and shallow, steep and level, sloping and flat, thick and thin. There should be different *weights*: wooden boxes, cardboard boxes, heavy and light objects. There should be toys with *divisible properties*, such as wood and clay. Others should have *porous properties*, such as water, paper, clothes, paper towels, sand, soil. Still others should have *compressible properties*, such as rubber balls, inflatable plastic animals, footprints in sand, pillows. Finally there should be some with *elastic properties*, such as balls and rubber bands.

In testing we distinguish *self-testing* from *social testing*. Some activities are trials for the self against nature, and some are trials for the self against other people.

EXAMPLES OF SELF-TESTING ACTIVITY

Activity	Places or Things That Help This Activity
Running	Clear open spaces, hand balls and footballs, wagons, planks raised from ground at one end to give running start
Throwing	Bean bags, hoops or boxes to throw balls into
Jumping	Bouncing board, jumping pit, low objects to step off
Climbing into, under, over	Stairs, jungle gym, rubber tires
Pedaling	Kiddy cars, tricycles
Pushing, pulling	Blocks, wagons
Hitting, punching	Punch bag
Kicking	Punch bag on string at slight height
Backing (down from or off)	Stairs, sofa
Supporting weight	Low horizontal bar
Swimming, splashing	Wading pool, bath
Balancing	Two-by-four beams on ground
Dancing	Floor space or carpet near record player

This is an exhaustive year of discovery and, even if earlier makeshift toys might do, this is a year for a new range of toys for babies to play with. The basic understanding of size, color, shape, texture, sound, movement, and position probably occurs very much as a result of the children's actions with available objects. Often the best toys are the available pots, pans, jars, cereal boxes, old towels, thread spools, wastepaper, and bath water. The filling and emptying of many containers with smaller objects is all-engrossing. It is the great age of filling and emptying.

We know also that the more toys children had in their first year, the more curious they will be in this one. There is a definite relationship between the variety of available objects in that year and the level of inquiry in this. There must be some limit on this relationship, but clearly some toys are better than none, even though most of us still hope that too *many* are not better than some. Being knee-deep in toys was never much fun for the parents.

Sometimes in this year there begins the long romance with recorded *music* and recorded marching. This may be done with your own stereo or with a child's own player. But marching and singing and dancing in time to music is everyone's right. There is a place also for repeating the commercials that are often heard on TV. Musical children pick these up and love them. They are not only sung, but also illustrated for them. It is amusing to see babies come rushing from one room as soon as they hear the strains of their favorite jingles. They stand there rigidly watching:

> Yum, yum Bumble-bee, Bumble-bee tuna,
> I love Bumble-bee, Bumble-bee tuna.

or

> You're the Bold one,
> You're the one for Bold,

Any commercial that has children in it really turns them on. Regardless of their content, the melody and rhythm of these commercials are as near as most of us will get to the repetitive rhythm of a tribal village or a folkway of life.

Most of the other types of toys have been listed under the activities of exploration and testing above, but we should again mention blocks and puzzles. We are talking here about the simple two- or three-part *puzzles*. We should remember that the purpose of a puzzle is not simply mastery but also play. After successfully putting the pieces together, most children at this age like to see what else they can do with them: stacking, twisting around, and laughing. Here is a very clearcut case where the additional time with the puzzle probably increases the child's understanding of its possibilities well beyond those intended by its maker.

During the first year babies' blankets and other accouterments have not been very noticeable. But some time in this or the next year a preference often develops for a *soft stuffed toy* or a *cuddly blanket*, rag, or diaper, which they like to have with them while feeding or going to bed. There has been quite a lot of psychological speculation about these items. They seem to carry some of the contact pleasures, smell pleasures, and sucking pleasures of early infancy, so they retain a continuity for children with that earlier period. At the same time they allow babies to reproduce these for themselves. They permit a transition from their passive earlier style to their more active way of life. With the "comforter" children can produce their own pleasures.

During the second year the teddy bear or soft toy seems to be a way of ensuring both dependence and independence. Babies can preserve independence of others by being alone with teddy. Soft toys continue to be used throughout childhood, and in recent years up through young adulthood. Their ambiguity allows them to be used for multiple purposes. They can be brought together as collections. They can be conversation pieces, a link between couples, a way of putting into make-believe sentiments that might be hard to express more directly, a target for aggression.

We now come to examples of social-testing activity. Games with adults, supported as they are by the adults' concern, exist in a special haven of life, which is itself not quite game and not quite nurturing alone. Games with other children at this age do not have this support. Two little children occasionally run (or chase, throw, or retrieve) more or less together or to and from each other. But these moments are partial and are not sustained unless an older child is really able to act with indulgence, as a parent would.

More typically, these one-year-olds will examine each other and test out what will happen. According to background and their own treatment they are as likely to hug the other as to hit the other, or they may react to the other's behavior by running, crying, or simply sitting and ignoring. More often than not they just watch each other. We might think of this as a form of *social testing*. It is behavior that will grow more important as children develop.

If you have played a lot with your babies, you will have given them the ingredients to allow them to participate in social play. A great deal of children's social life in the years to come will be the setting up of pecking orders. To the extent that they can play games together, however, they will have discovered ways of changing raw power struggles into rule-controlled activities.

Differences between Mastery and Play

Mastery is not play. We have been using the words "mastery" and "play" differently in our descriptions above. It is time to explain what we mean. Earlier we described games and play as involving a special state of being at ease, in control, and abstracted from the surrounding world. But there are many things that children do with their time that are not play, and we wish now to discuss these.

Play is not urgent behavior. Even in the first months of life we can see that babies act urgently, even frantically, during feeding. They snort through their noses and vigorously move their hands and legs. Then, as they get their first mouthfuls of food, they quiet down, although they continue to suck vigorously. Here babies respond to the urgent demands of their bodies and do whatever is necessary to meet these needs. This is also true for other urgent needs like trying to get warm, remove pain, or avoid noise.

In general, those who are suffering such urgencies cannot play. They must get rid of discomfort before they can play. There are occasionally exceptions; for example, when children become so preoccupied with their play that they forget to relieve themselves, when they put up with scratches and bruises because they are so involved in the game, or when they do not want to come in to dinner because they are having too much fun. These instances, however, usually occur at a later age, when the excitement that children can get from their play has already been well learned. In the first year that kind of exception does not come up. Babies play when the other urgencies are done with.

Play is not mastery. The difference between play and mastery is not generally understood. It is one of the most important distinctions that we will make in this book. Mastery means the same thing as *work*, and to say that play is not mastery is to say that play is not work, which is obvious. Yet such has been our Western civilization's neglect of "childish" things over the centuries, such has been our feeling that anything children do is trivial, that we have tended to call everything children do "play." Because their actions did not contribute to the moneymaking of the world, it was not work. Not being work, it must be play.

But this does not follow. You work at something whenever your present actions are carried out primarily in order to lead to some end result. The results in our adult cases are salaries, promotions, products, fame, prestige, inventions, creations, etc. Most of children's free activity is of this sort. They spend most of their time trying to find out how to get results by their own activity. After feeding, for example, they spend much time examining the nipple with their mouths and their fingers. They push it this way and that way. They want to find out what produces what results. What must they do to get it under their tongues? What must they do to get it under their lips? They want results. This is work; but because it does not produce a salary, fame, or prestige, we use another name for it, and that name is mastery. There is also an important distinction between the results children have in mind and the results adults are pursuing. Children carry out their work to understand; adults carry out theirs to survive.

Mastery is work. Most of children's free activity is concerned with mastering things or people. This highly serious activity results in children's adjusting to their surroundings. They work at it night and day. They explore all the objects they can find. They explore their homes and their back yards. They attempt to manipulate other children into playing with them in their own way. They do their best to get their parents to do what they want. They do their best to act as their parents do. The greater part of childhood is passed in learning the art of mastery.

In the first several years of life it is not very easy to tell the difference between mastery activities and play because we cannot always see what results children have in mind. Without knowing what they have in mind, we cannot always make these distinctions. For this reason the two are mixed together in the early chapters of this book. We make no excuses for this. Until we have much better records (videotape and film) of young children's behavior, we will not be able to tell these differences easily.

In the past those educators who advocated the "playway" of schooling were generally talking about mastery, not about play. They wanted the schools to be places where children would be free to discover and to learn from the materials that they provided; but it was work freely pursued, or mastery, that they had in mind, not play.

6 | On the Importance of Only Pretending:

From Two to Three Years

"Daddy, will you play ball with me?"
"No, I'm busy. . . . All right, you can go outside." [It was snowing.]

•

"I'm not yours.
I'm not your child.
You can't wear my new white shirt.
This house doesn't belong to you."

•

"Who is that in the mirror?"
"Mary." [Age two and one-half.]
"Will she be there when you go?"
"Yes."
"Why?"
"Cause she can't get out. She would break the mirror."

Two-year-olds have problems determining who they are. What are their selves, and what are not? What are their choices, and what are not? Children become concerned with their self-identities, at about eighteen months. These feelings persist through the third year. It is better to cooperate with your children and help them now, rather than to give them orders. This goes for eating, toilet training, going to bed, getting dressed, and going to sleep, which are often crises for many parents during this second to third year.

Children's sensitivity about themselves is often expressed in their concern over what they are named. "I am not a baby. I am a little girl," they may say; although at a later time, when it fits a mood of greater dependency, they might well say the opposite, "I am a baby. I am not a little girl." The wise parent is able to accommodate these needs, to allow independence when it is wise and to give comfort when it is needed.

Actually, what strikes most parents about this age is children's great capacity for independent movement. Two- to three-year-olds, or *toddlers*, are everywhere and often are in great danger, because they have no appreciation of what might happen to them. They may run full tilt into objects. They want to dress and undress themselves. They want to organize their own toys, clothes, and books. They may carry about little piles of books for you to read to them. They begin to show some sort of distinctive personality. They are vigorous or timid, loving or detached, very interested in people or mainly interested in their toys, and so on.

But from the point of view of play the most interesting thing about this third year is that the new awareness of self and the new capacity for language, which create negativism, also create an awareness of *only pretending*. Pretense is the play milestone for this year.

We need to make clear that even during the previous year there will have been some make-believe play with dolls and trucks that we might call pretending, but babies do not have that idea yet. During the prior year they may practice *imitating* adults by playing with dolls and trucks, but they do not yet call it pretending. It is having a name for what they do in this third year that gives them a whole lot more freedom than they had before. Pretending can take them anywhere.

Children of two to three move easily in and out of pretense if they are allowed to. At one moment they are cowboys, at another they are themselves. The very flexibility of the boundaries between being cowboys and being themselves appears to be a great help to them in growing up to be what they want to be as well as what they have to be. At the very least the word "pretend" gives children a useful defense, so they can obtain the right to be left alone when they are working things through for themselves. If we ask a question and they say "I'm just pretending," it is important not to push them. Do not ridicule them. Just leave them to their privacy. When children are given space in which to pretend, it seems to make them optimistic. Children who can pretend can also believe.

The act of pretending should not be taken for granted. In many cultures, children are treated in a most authoritarian and confining way. The adults live on the fringe of economic uncertainty, and there is little scope for changing their lives. Here a widespread attitude of fatalism prevails. There is an unwillingness to believe that one's own actions can alter life or one's circumstances in any way. There is little scope for a belief in pretend play in such places.

We would seriously suggest that two-year-olds who can intersperse the optimistic banner of pretense through much of their everyday activities are adjusting to them without giving up hope, courage, optimism, and the belief in possible worlds. What may seem an annoyance or even a lie to the adult may be pure optimistic character development for children.

This optimistic character-forming function of pretending may not be obvious to all, because of our past habits of training most children for routine work. Civilization is only now beginning to think about the problem of training children for creative work. The same negative attitude toward pretending has existed in psychology also. The psychologists who have had the most to say about such things as pretense, daydreams, imagination, wishes, and dreams have been mainly concerned with abnormal psychology. They have observed the way in which an abnormal person is often trapped in his daydreams, and they have thought of his daydreams and pretending as a defense against adjusting more adequately, when they were really a last-ditch effort to be human. Recent research, however, has shown that normal people daydream and pretend also. In fact, they have richer daydreams (though less repetitive ones).

In the fourth year many children will, for example, create imaginary companions. They have no one to play with, and they tend to be children with initiative; therefore they create their own playmates to remedy the situation. This is not to be lamented. It is a sign of considerable resourcefulness. When adults do this sort of thing with creative competence, we call them novelists or dramatists. Along with children they have the desire to create new worlds, just as real, but *other* than, the one that is.

It pays then to think of pretense as a poetry of possibility playing around the edges of necessary fact. If we realize that the third year is when children become indubitably selves, with a name, and refer to themselves as *I* and yet also come to realize that they are relatively powerless and small and have relatively little say in most events, we also realize that they will have a need to buttress their confidence with thoughts of the way things might be. Pretense is both a natural power and a power in adversity.

GAMES AND OTHER THINGS TO DO

In this year many of the games will be brought to you by your children. Most of the time they are taking the initiative, and your role is often to respond rather than to begin things as you did in the first year.

Interludes

Interludes are the mixing of play with ordinary activities. Inter means "between." Ludus is Latin for "play." Interludes are plays in between. In the middle of your vacuuming your little child will suddenly appear with a suitcase and, going to the door, will wave good-bye. "I'm going to the hospital. Good-bye, Good-bye." This small act of leaving may be repeated twenty times. Your role is to enter into the play just a little but not too much. Wave good-bye but go on vacuuming. Wave good-bye and make a mock crying face but then go on with your vacuuming. Finally go to him and ask, "Have you come home now?" "Yes," he replies. Then hug him to pieces, exclaiming how happy you are.

This little game, like many others, is likely to crop up particularly if you have been leaving home a lot and have not been able to take him. The game represents the child's reversal of the circumstances. Now *he* leaves, and *you* stay home. But of course all he wants to consider is the possibility; he certainly does not want to lose you. If he really should leave, then he would lose you. So you play with the game around the edges and do not respond with such belief that the child is forced to go through with it almost as a reality. An error made by some adults is to take a child's pretenses so seriously that the child is more frightened by a pretense than by reality.

We have to understand that *power through play* always means turning life about-face, so that those who were powerless are now powerful. We spoke earlier of children who were concerned with mastery or accommodating themselves and eventually learning to control circumstances. But the players always rise above circumstances, which means they *reverse* their customary relationship with them. It is difficult to understand play without this idea of reversibility.

Other *interludes* of children may have to do with dangerous or frightening things they have merely witnessed, such as an elephant in the circus, a monster on "Sesame Street," or a crab in a picture book. The usual procedure is for children to react to the danger sometime later by reversing the situation and becoming the thing that frightens them. "I'm an elephant," they cry. Your cries of mock fear are a good response. "Oh, I'm going to get squashed," you cry. You can have some roughhouse fun on the floor here or, if not, you can pretend to be scared and then laugh with them as they laugh at your exaggerated reaction. Your reaction to their threat is in a sense something like their original fear. So you have helped by reversing the roles and becoming the helpless child. They have acted powerfully. You have acted powerlessly.

Other interludes have more to do with simpler things, like wishes. "Let's take Barbie to the store. Let's buy her some shoes," says your baby daughter. In this one suggestion she wants to go to the store, and she wants to get some shoes. But Barbie (the doll) is the pretend one who prompts the suggestion. "Well," you say, "she has such small feet. We could buy her a hundred pairs." Usually further playful discussion follows. If it does not, and the child wants to go, and go now, then you shift gears into reality. You come back to whatever makes sense for you: "We're going tomorrow" or "You don't need shoes" or "Let's go."

Reports

Increasingly you are asked to be responsive to *reports* of visits, to Santa Claus or wherever they have been lately. These reports are mixtures of expressive acting out, some words, and some small sentences that they can speak by now. Since their expressions and words are sometimes ahead of their full understanding of what they are saying, it often sounds quaint. But to be a good listener is a very important part of this game, and since you can be that while you go on with other things, the expense in time may not be too great.

Dinner time and the captive audience, as well as the desire to get in on the conversational act, prompt them to an endless discourse on how Santa will come down the chimney or whatever. Younger babies enjoy the dinner-time social hour. We remember our youngest daughter holding forth loudly "talking" while the older children talked about school. Sometimes she drowned us all out, no small feat against six other talkers. They will also enjoy *your* "reports" of their activities at an earlier period; that is, their personal history.

Chasing

Chasing has become embellished. They can now both chase and be chased, although this is generally a one-to-one-person game. But now they may chase you, with hands outstretched and with Frankenstein grasp and monster face. There are many new faces this year. They can pretend to cry and to be angry. We have added the *mask* of drama. In addition, they may put their heads down and pretend to be counting. If they are regular "Sesame Street" fans, they may know some numbers. Some children indeed can count right through to ten at this age. It is of the same order as being able to sing "ABC," which some can do. In both cases they are known by rote.

Another part of the game is to pretend not to see someone when they know where they are hiding. Then again there is a surprise peek-a-boo type of ending, where they say, "They're not there; they're not there; there they are!" with great acclaim. As before we are both still *acting out* this game rather than playing it. All our social games with babies and young children seem to be as much like dramas as they are like games.

Being an Audience

You have a performer on your hands. The game is to watch and enjoy. It may be gymnastics. Babies somersault with the help of older brothers or sisters (once-over on the carpet). They *sing*. In the singing family you will have been singing with them a whole host of favorites, including "Jack and Jill," "*Frère Jacques*," "Twinkle, Twinkle," "ABC," and, the most important of all, "Happy Birthday." And we should not forget the TV commercials. Snatches of these will appear off and on continually in the life of the frequent television watcher. They *dance*. Now with a scarf in their hands they do not look unlike Isadora, or in a different mood they do straight-out mod rock.

Ring Games

It is a little early for ring games, but where there are older brothers and sisters, "Ring Around the Rosy" produces great excitement, particularly falling on the floor at the end.

Ring around the rosy,
A pocket full of posies,
Ashes, ashes,
We all fall down.

A ring game of this sort, as well as chasing, does not come fully into children's repertoires until they are about four. If you or other children play this with them frequently, however, they will pick up a great deal of its character, even if they do not understand the whole game.

It is difficult to avoid the conclusion that much of learning is in the first play imitation. In nearly all games with older persons, the younger player has only an idea of what is really involved, and yet with help they are able to make a reasonable response for some years before their ability matches their performance.

The more active two-and-one-half-year-olds can play other *circle* pantomime games, where everyone does the same thing together. These are games where everyone acts their way through the weekday routines together, for example, "This is the way we go to the store," "This is the way we watch TV," "This is the way we wash the clothes," etc.; but two-year-olds can only really participate if there are a group of elders for them to hold hands with, "On a cold and frosty morning." But we will have more to say of these circle games in the next chapter.

Find My Hand

Even last year's game of looking for objects gets reversed. Now they are asking you to find their hands, which are buried under the newspaper, behind their backs, or wherever. Why is the pretense of not finding, of almost finding, and then of finally finding, with loud triumph, so much fun? So much of what we have called games throughout these chapters is really the *pretense of games*. Essentially we reduce the apparent game (hunt the finger, hunt the slipper) to the simpler anticipation game of surprise. We are pretending a game on a higher level but actually playing one on a lower level. The name of the game may be hide and seek, but the real game is anticipation and surprise.

Picture Misnaming

You may have begun telling them the stories of "Goldilocks and the Three Bears" or "The Three Little Pigs," although they may not be ready for that yet. Still, they will certainly be very ready next year, so there is no reason not to try and see how it goes. Usually you will do well with picture books and straightforward accounts of people, houses, and other things around them. In other words it is the descriptions of their familiar world that they like this year, rather than the story.

On the story level we are still into imitating everyday life. Children can name many things now, such as colors, numbers, and animals. That is partly the pleasure of going through books with them. What we can do for fun, however, is make foolish mistakes; for example, we can say, "Hey, here's a lion," when we know it is a horse, and then, "Oh, my mistake." When this is done gradually, it can lead to riotous games of misnaming. But, again, do not proceed unless they enjoy the joke. In due course they will be making them themselves. This is a preparation for next year's mangled nursery rhymes.

We should add here, though, that as stories are begun,

children do by and large like them straight. At this age routine, order, and continuity are ways in which children borrow a stable ego from the world in which they live. Our child can get very annoyed if you do not tell the story in the same way and in the same place at the same time. This should be respected for a while; then you can suggest alternatives. Be flexible but not absurd. It is easy to act farfetched for one's own amusement, but in the process one can completely bewilder a child.

For children who do appreciate stories ("Goldilocks and the Three Bears," "The Three Little Pigs," "Red Riding Hood"), they can join in more and more. The child puts in the noises of the animals or adds the words; thus, "This is a story about three . . ." and the child shouts "bears!" Throughout the story gaps are presented and questions are asked. This type of technique, carried on for the next year or so, finally gives you a situation where, in effect, you carry the scenario, but the child tells most of the story. The story becomes a dialogue for two, with noises and much wild invention. Do not miss this kind of fun.

Follow the Leader

The game of follow the leader can take multiple forms. It can be activities around the backyard or in the sitting room, such as walking, sitting down, balancing on one foot, hopping with two feet, skipping (all very hard at this age); it can be pretend actions, such as sleeping, telephoning, washing your face, putting on clothes; or it can be small motor acts, such as opening and closing your hand, mouth, or eyes or drumming with your fingers. Three-year-olds love games of this sort. The amazing thing is how few of them they get.

Hide the "What Is It?"

Hide the "what is it?" is every form of hiding and *naming*. It is really a word game. You may hide a part of the body or an object, and the child has to guess what it is that is hidden. The game progresses from the obvious things, like your hand, to smaller objects that have been standing nearby. A variation of the game is to have the child guess what an object is just by feeling it.

Destruction

Breaking up sand castles, jumping on them, bashing down block towers, and smashing down block houses are naturals for destruction. You build them, and they destroy them; or you both build, and you both destroy. In part, this destruction is the natural opposite to a long period of concentrated construction that you first begin to see signs of in this third year. Constructing takes much hard work and self-control. It is not strange that it leads to its opposite. It was mastery to do it one way, and it is fun to do it the other. Probably the wise recommendation is for *both* of you to build and for *both* of you to destroy. You should not see this simply as aggression, although aggressive force is involved. Destruction is also liberation. It is a new beginning again. It is the thing that all artists must learn if they are to progress. We are caught by our own conventions. Some modern ideas in art have destruction as the keynote. Make your art object; tear it to pieces; and make something new out of the pieces. Too often we have been so frightened by destruction and violence that we have not been able to see the essential function of demolition in creative rebuilding.

THE CHILD'S OWN PLAY

At this age, as before, we have much to say about exploration and testing again. They become more sophisticated. But the really new event in children's play is pretending to imitate other people.

Exploration and Testing: Activities and Materials

The exploratory play of two-year-olds was simple and piecemeal. Play now becomes more a part of *combinations* and *building*. There is more novelty in the combinations of motor elements. They can manipulate and watch the results at the same time. It is a big step from the direct use of their hands to using tools. Still, certain major *actions* occupy much of their time, as the following list shows.

EXAMPLES OF EXPLORATORY ACTIVITY

Activity	Tools
Combining	Counters, blocks
Molding	Clay, play dough
Spreading	Sand
Heaping	Blocks
Squeezing, making holes	Clay
Breaking, mending	Clay, silly putty
Using tools (sticks, etc.)	Clay
Finger painting	Water-soluble paints
Crayoning poster colors	Easels
Stringing	Wooden beads
Scissoring	Paper, scissors
Lacing	Cards with holes
Fitting puzzles	Geometrically shaped pieces, animal-shaped cutouts, peg boards

Recommended objects are egg beaters, linking blocks (for trains), water, sponges, pans, soapsuds, soda straws, bubble pipes, floating toys, clay, flexible plastic for cutting out, and cigar-box blocks.

With testing all of the second-year tests are still important: running, throwing, jumping, climbing, pedaling, pushing, pulling, hitting, punching, picking, balancing, and splashing. But instead of running at large and climbing only simple steps children can now perform these and other tests at a higher and more specific level. For example, they can climb onto a narrow space or seat, walk a line heel to toe, hop two or three steps on one foot, walk on a balance beam, throw a ball about ten feet, hang by their arms from low parallel bars, march and dance to records, roll down grass slopes, jump in puddles and on sand castles, and do simple gymnastics like somersaults.

There are even more toys that are useful now. There are three-piece puzzles, hole-punches, drinking straws, pipe cleaners, hand puppets, clay, tricycles, bean bags, swings, slides, painting and drawing materials, play dough, blocks that interlock, egg beaters, bubble pipes, soap suds, water, finger paints, poster paints, parallel bars, tunnels, plank bridges, packing cases, cardboard boxes inside cardboard boxes, wheelbarrows, pull and push cars or wagons, beads, shoelaces, pebbles, miniature playing cards, marbles, and buttons; toy scissors are also manageable.

Regarding social testing with other children, at this age children are often desperately eager to be with other children but not usually very adequate at managing the play situation. What they usually try to do is to get adults to help them. Even while in the midst of other children they will be urging the adult in charge to look at what they are doing, help them with their play, play with them, and/or chase them; or they will be urging you to intervene on their behalf with the other children to make the others do what they want, give them the toy they want, and/or make them leave them alone.

It is an interesting time, in which although drawn to other children, they still find adults more important, and they use adults as a bridge to the other children. One of the best solutions to this problem is for the adult actually to participate in their play. A careful adult can foster play in groups of children through participation in make-believe, and yet the individual children can at the same time be safeguarded from the excesses of each other.

We have to be careful in how we participate at this early age. Most adults are not particularly good at this. They are so self-conscious about their "baby" behavior that they may overact in the role, either acting in too grown up and sensible a way, like a lecturer, or indulging their own infantile selves in baby talk. Our advice is to take it easy. Sit on the floor quietly. Intrude only occasionally, with a mild example here and there—for example, by rocking the doll or building with the blocks—all the time being very responsive to the children's imaginative suggestions that will keep the play going.

The problem is that this is the period of life that most of us have pretty nearly forgotten. We come back to it like complete strangers who may well act adult-centered in making false steps. Imagine yourself in China or Japan as a friend of the host. You are living in a house, all of whose customs are very strange, but you dearly wish to create a favorable impression. A similar tentativeness with respect to joining in the group play of two- to three-year-olds will serve you well. To ignore these precautions is perhaps to plunge in with the sins of your own childhood showing, whatever they may be.

We should perhaps point out that we are here talking about participating with children at their childish level, unlike the games mentioned earlier, where we were concerned with lifting them to our own level.

Often children at this age do very well when they are

"bossed" by older children and become babies when they play house. It is good for them, even if they are restricted in the roles they get to play. Here at least they can see the roles of the older child. Also, just as in the examples of chasing we have given previously, they have to learn one side of these reciprocal roles (parent or baby) before they can learn the other.

Occasionally small groups of two-year-olds play quite well together without the help of elders. This is usually when there is plenty of space and plenty of toys. It is more often outdoors. The space and the play objects allow them to get away from each other if necessary. Again with tunnels or hills, occasionally they will do things in parallel fashion with great enjoyment, all rolling down the hill or running in sequence through the tunnel. These events do not happen too often though.

Imitation

We have said that this is the year for beginning to pretend. The earliest pretense takes the form of imitation. Imitation is learning by paying attention to what other people do. *Imitation is a form of mastery.* This route to knowledge—copying what others do—has always been the way to learn social behavior. We see this in children's first gestures, their first expressions ("good-bye") and words ("Mommy"), which are taken directly from their parents. It is not until the second year that they copy their parents more carefully. Children who can now walk and run about try to do what they see their parents do. They try to sweep with brooms, to wash dishes, to turn on ovens, or to drive cars. Naturally you have to interfere quite a bit; they are too small or it may be too dangerous. But it is still the basic way children learn from their parents.

ROSENFELD ASSOCIATES

MYRON E. ROSENFELD, M.D.

ELKINS PARK HOUSE   SUITE 111-B

7900 OLD YORK ROAD

ELKINS PARK, PENNSYLVANIA 19117

885-5580

℞

Luci Harp

Selsun Suspension

Disp # 120/

Sig: Shampoo as directed

NOT TO BE RENEWED

Many formal systems of education are based almost completely on imitating the teacher. In general, it seems that the more authoritarian the family or the society, the more it tends to rely on teaching children this way. In more open and flexible societies children get to do more on their own. There are wide individual differences in the use of this form of mastery. Some children spend most of their time at first in imitative play, then later in the more advanced form of imitation, which is dramatic play with other children.

The modern world forces imitative play. Actually our modern world is so complex and so dangerous that we have made children imitate us less and play more. We have forced them away from mastery of the actual environment (imitative mastery) and have given them mastery of toys and play with toys instead (imitative play). The billions of dollars that we spend on toys and models, which are miniatures of the world, is unheard of in human history. We do not want our preschool children to try to master our cars, our ovens, and our roadways. "No, you can't wash the dishes, you'll break them." Instead, when they are two or three, we give them a toy tea set and let them wash the dishes in a small pail of water. We take the broom from them because they have just accidentally hit us on the head with the handle and insist that they play with their toy house set.

So we definitely push for toys as among the only forms of mastery we allow. Naturally children like them, and they are of some appeal to all of us because at least with them we can feel in control, can be relaxed, and can handle them our way. But by pushing for so much use of toys we are doing something special to human nature. Instead of having competent little aborigines who are masters of their physical and social worlds, who can survive fairly well even when quite young, we have children who have acquired many many alphabets of toys and play but are completely dependent on their elders for survival for many years to come.

What does it do when you have a head full of toys instead of a head full of animal tracks? As we proceed in the chapters ahead, perhaps we can answer that question.

Toward the end of the second year we see the first signs of imitative play. Children pretend to sleep on the carpet or they pretend to drink with a block. They call the block a cup. By the time they are in their third year, they are making their teddy bears or dolls take a drink. Usually they put their dolls through much the same routines that they must go through themselves. The teddy bear is put to bed, is put on the pot, is given a drink, etc.

Later in this same year they become the actors in their own imitative play. Thus, children are the mothers and fathers, and the doll is the baby. At these early stages they seem to be helped by having toys that represent the people and activities that they wish to imitate. Increasingly elements of feeling enter their play, so we can no longer speak of imitation but must call the activity make-believe. The parents now spank the babies, and the babies act as if they are naughty. This is usually a statement of what they feel might happen or what they feel they would like to do rather than any strict imitation.

What impresses us about these pretend imitations and make-believe plays, however, is that children can represent their lives and feelings more completely here than in any other way. They are not able to make such a complete statement of the way they feel in words. They certainly cannot make it in their drawings. As a form of self-representation play is therefore far ahead of these other forms of expression. Apparently play not only gives them a chance to be flexible because they have the power but also allows them to make a statement about what their world means more fully than they can do anywhere else.

At the end of this book in an appendix we have listed in much greater detail the steps that we think children go through first in imitative play and later in games. A scale of this sort is most valuable for parents or nursery school workers who want to have some way of knowing just where their child is in his development. Or of knowing after they have been training him in some way whether they have brought about any change in his level of imaginative play.

7 The Future of Make-Believe:
From Three to Four Years

"I'm going to get big and you're going to get little," he says.
"What will you do to me when I get little?"
"I'll put your coat on."

•

"Why do you like playing with dolls?"
"If they are bad you can spank them. If they're real bad you can stick a pin in them. And you couldn't do that with babies cause they've got real tender bottoms."

•

He burps.
"What's that?" we ask.
"A fart of the throw-up," he replies.

•

"Yesternight I dreamed that Daddy fell over and hit his head on the table."

•

"I have a cut on my eye. That's why I fell over."

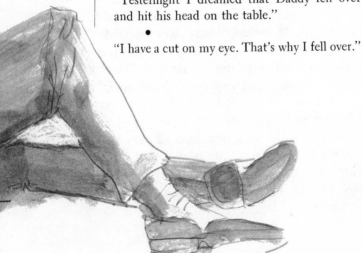

Three to four years of age is a fairly stable period for a child. In the two preceding years you and your child have more or less ironed out your mutual family relationships. Children at this age have developed considerable competence in moving around (they can skip, jump, and run smoothly), and they are capable now with the smaller movements of threading, building blocks, and drawing. They can use pencils, paints, crayons, and paper in the ways they are supposed to be used. They are more efficient in dressing, eating, toileting, social exchanges, and talking. This is a year for much, although not very logical, talking.

Not surprisingly, the first forms of child-to-child social life begin to take place. Children create their first societies. In addition, the beginning of group play raises the question of play management—of who shall be boss and who shall be bossed.

Some children take important steps ahead in make-believe play and some do not, which raises the question of whether make-believe should be taught to those who do not use it very well. This is a revolutionary notion. People have often thought play to be useless. Those who thought it to be valuable felt that it was instinctive and that all the child needed was privacy and perhaps some equipment. We have suggested that playing games with your baby from birth is legitimate. Now we add the even more heretical suggestion that children might have to be coached in make-believe play.

Some children rise to a new level of play in this year that takes them beyond exploration and testing, beyond even imitation—namely, play *construction*. In addition to their social play, play construction is the play milestone for three- to four-year-olds.

GAMES AND OTHER THINGS TO DO

The games that follow are impressive for the increasing flexibility that they demand and for the reversals that occur in the players and in the moves they make.

Role Reversal

Now that children can pretend to be adults, fathers, or mothers in their own play and can portray some of the feelings of those adults, they can also accept and enjoy your pretending to be a child. At this age children are not particularly clear on the reversibility or irreversibility of age differences in any case. At this time television adds to the confusion by making grown-ups appear to be little. A popular child-image at this age is that there are little people inside the television box.

It is fun for the parent to pretend to be small and to be ordered about by the child, particularly since the parent can be disobedient and naughty, although it is important in these games not to become too powerful, even in the inferior role. Power is to be diminished, not exaggerated. You may have to set limits if the child becomes too tyrannical. The aim is humorous role switching. "I told you to eat the carpet." "I can't, cause I just turned into a sleeping dog." The general rule is that it is all pretending. "I *am* eating the carpet. I'm pretending." A danger is that you will be utterly superior, even in role switching, and it may be a further case of one-upmanship rather than shared play.

Story Dialogues

You have been and are still telling many stories in a fairly conventional way. You repeat them and repeat them and repeat them. But one way to make them more fun at this age is to make a dialogue out of them. "There were three bears, and then what happened?" A more advanced step is to have children tell you the story. This a marvelous event because the retelling is usually quite selective and tells you much about what they enjoy.

Our four-year-old loves "Hansel and Gretel," but what she always remembers first and cares about most is when they eat the candy off the old witch's house. The notion of a house made of candy is simply too much. In "Goldilocks and the Three Bears" she remembers the broken chair that Goldilocks sat in. She hurt her bottom when it broke. After the child has fallen off her chair countless times and hurt *her* bottom, this interest is not surprising. In "The Three Little Pigs" she delights in the wolf's coming down the chimney. Why, we do not know. In "Snow White" it is the prince—the prince all the way—and so much for those cunning little dwarfs.

Another possibility for these stories is to act them out together. The beach is a good place for this. Snow White is carried off by the witch and then rescued by the prince. Older brothers and sisters, as well as parents, can play the supporting roles, while the four-year-old is the princess or prince, the triumphant heroine or hero. This is like living out a fairy tale and completely fascinates three- or four-year-olds.

An important note in this day and age is that when you tell a folk story, try to make the hero or heroine the same sex as your child. In "Hansel and Gretel," if you tell it to a girl, Gretel can be the one who has the idea of dropping stones and crumbs to find the way home and ends up pushing the witch into the oven. In "Goldilocks and the Three Bears" there is no reason why the appealing little baby bear cannot be a girl bear. It is an unfortunate fact about fairy tales that the heroines usually get their rewards only by being rather sweet and having magic come their way—be sweet and your prince will come. But as we have emphasized throughout, you can be as flexible with fairy tales as with anything else. After you have read these stories once to refresh your memory, it is better thereafter to tell them yourself.

At the same time do not be too embarrassed about some magic here. This is a preschool age, and one needs a sense of being protected, of good things happening, of being in a good world. Do not expect your child to want to be a fully grown person yet, a feminist for example. That can be scary also, because it imposes burdens when your child is still too young. Children at this age want to feel that they can protect others and that they will be protected. Unfortunately many of them get only the message that they are helpless and will not be protected, to which they react by feeling completely inadequate or by being very aggressive and hostile. So do not underestimate the *benevolence* and magic in fairy tales; it is important at this age.

Board and Card Games

Children cannot really understand board and card games yet, but they can enjoy "playing" at playing them with you. They give you half the pack, and you each take a turn at putting down a card, which they then put somewhere else. You can assist in minor ways by picking the cards up and dividing them. Sometimes they partly understand you when you sort reds and blacks, but they cannot do it consistently. Likewise with board games there is a certain amount of throwing dice, counting the dots, sorting the counters, tracing the journey on the Parcheesi board, etc. They feel that they are playing the game. Similarly they can roll marbles around and store them in containers, and because they appear like other players, they feel that they are playing a game. But in our terms it is mainly a mastery exercise in the mystery of these properties—rolling them around, seeing what they will do, etc. Sometimes the throwing or rolling will excite them, and they will laugh and get involved in their own game.

Hide and Seek

You are both really taking turns at hiding and seeking now, but children do not really understand you as the seeker when they are the hider or you as the hider when they are the seeker. Thus, they get upset if they cannot find you fairly quickly, and they wander out of their hiding places when you are supposed to be seeking. Still, much of the time the finding and hiding, even though they only partly understand it all, are fun.

Telephone Conversations

Just as a dialogue between you and the child becomes more possible in the telling of stories, such dialogues are even easier with toy or pretend telephones. You can talk about the events of the day, and requests for immediate help in an accident are common content. Further, you can call "others" to the phone and imitate other voices, so that everything gets hilarious after a bit.

Races

You can race with children now. They race a tricycle; you use a four-legged crawl. First to touch the door wins. But you never win—you keep falling over, or you get a pin in your hand—anything. Competition is too intense and loss is too overwhelming yet for you to win, but you can draw.

Winning and Losing

There are some parents who cannot wait to get on with the competition—the winning and losing. There are others who abominate the competitive system and think if we could cut out all winning and losing, that would be the end of war and the atom bomb. Either way, let us postpone the issue until about the age of seven years. Losing experiences carry too much weight in these early years; they are overwhelming. The adults who think it is OK generally are not very sensitive to the needs and feelings of those around them. They are the ones who throw children in the water to get them used to it. This kind of thing does not always fail, but it usually does. The odds are against its helping much. Having fun together and trusting and believing in one's playmates are probably a better basis for building courage at a later age. At this point you are the reassuring playmate.

TEACHING PLAY

Up to this point we have been playing or teaching games that have been above the level of the child's own solitary play. The question whether we shouldn't also play with children *at*, rather than *above*, their own level of play has been raised by those who are worried that some children are not developing their imaginative powers to a sufficient extent.

In the last chapter we talked about participating in children's make-believe play. This is something that intelligent parents and nursery school teachers have always done to some extent. In recent years, however, the suggestion has been made that there are large groups of disadvantaged children who do not engage in make-believe play and who should be taught to do so; otherwise they will not develop their imaginative powers. Since the whole theme of this book has to do with playing with children in various ways (through games and through their own make-believe), for us this is a central issue. Although we talk here mainly of children in nursery school, kindergarten, or day-care centers, what we have to say applies equally well to parents who are concerned with knowing just where their own child's play level is and how to play with the child beginning at that level.

Is it possible that make-believe and imagination are not universal? It hardly seems so. We know that every human culture is a creative product. Each culture is like a "human" experiment in being alive at a certain time and in a certain place, and the responses to that problem have varied most widely from place to place. Now what we call imagination in modern society or, in the present case, make-believe play is something we have come to identify as the result of the writings of people highly gifted in fantasy (Lewis Carroll, James Barrie, Walt Disney) and the result of writers famous in the nursery school movement (Friedrich Frobel, Susan Isaacs). Whether these people meant to make it this way or not, the common-sense notion of make-believe play used these days means playing with dolls, houses, blocks, and trucks in a playroom. A sceptic would say that this is make-believe adapted to living in a comfortable suburban house, tucked away at a safe distance from the rigors of the outdoor world and the dangers from the people of the streets.

Because most modern psychologists have been brought up in this tradition, they have tended to assume that if children did not play this way, then they did not play at all. Yet this is clearly not true. The anthropological record shows that there are many different ways of playing and many different kinds of games. Children do not all grow up the same way. There is no single language of play. There are many foreign languages of play. There are groups that do not have any of the games that we regard as so natural.

Let us look for a moment at the Australian aborigines, who have many imaginative games. These groups have often been said to be the most "primitive." Perhaps what is really meant by that is that their struggle for survival has been sufficiently difficult that they have had little time left for the kinds of development that we regard as complex. The evidence is however that many of their terminologies for plants, animals, and social relationships are just as complex as ours.

Their play is indeed a long catalog of preparation for tracking, tree climbing, canoeing, hunting, spearing, animal identification, boomeranging, fighting, swimming, marriage and family, cooking, fire making, corroborees, sand drawing, storytelling, singing, string figures, memory training, and mimicry. There are very high requirements for *mastery* in exploration, testing, and imitation.

Thus, in historical aboriginal Australia adults reward children who make the best imitations of kangaroos, emus or other birds, iguanas, tortoises, cockatoos, and crocodiles. Adults reproduce with great care the various forms of animal tracks. The children are encouraged to imitate them and are praised or criticized accordingly by their elders. The foot tracks of individual tribe members are also practiced. It is not unusual for a mother to "lose" her child away from camp and so make the child find her tracks and follow her home.

The children have to know what their natural world is like and how it functions, and they have to know who they are and what they can do in relation to their world if they are to survive. But in many cases there is a playful and "imaginative" extension of these forms of mastery. Even the most important of tribal festivals, the corroboree, is imitative. The boys paint their bodies and perform their mimicry of dances for the younger children. Clowning and individual wit are as valued as in the true ceremony. At the other end of the scale children make playthings of frogs tied by the legs or iguanas tied by the tail. Even carpet snakes, with their teeth rubbed down, are treated as pets.

In a game of water birds one child, unseen by the others, hides himself at the water's edge and imitates the call of a particular bird. The others must use their hunting skills to attempt to "catch" the bird, and the mimic has to try to escape using only the physical actions of the bird. To do this he might dive under the water, surfacing with his head covered with duck weed in imitation of various water birds and animals. Now clearly in games like this one the imagination is disciplined by the requirements of the game, but it is hard to deny either that the game as a whole is an imaginative exercise or that in the course of the game considerable make-believe elaboration is required by the central player.

The situation is much like that in those parts of the modern world where children grow up with adults for whom physical skill is still their major mode of living. Children who grow up on farms, for example, spend most of their mastery time and playtime perfecting physical skills. They physically explore their environment and physically test themselves against it. They are imitating their hunting and laboring fathers and mothers.

For poverty children who grow up in city streets there is the additional need to do battle against all the other deprived. The struggle for survival involves doing physical battle with others on a day-to-day basis. The greater proportion of mastery focuses on these urgent matters. When there is scope for play (some free time, some familiarity, some safety), it centers upon the same issues. There is chasing and fighting of a mock character.

What has shocked many middle-class nursery school teachers dealing for the first time with poverty children or those from homes where physical struggle is the essence of survival is that these children do not fit in very easily with the middle-class, carpeted, and sedentary climate of the nursery school.

They do not know what to do there. Often they fight over toys. They are relatively at home outdoors with tricycles, jungle gyms, racing about, jumping, climbing, chasing, and fighting, but they do not have much use for blocks, sand, water, or playing house.

Some teachers think, therefore, that these children are without imagination. But as we have been demonstrating, this is not completely true. The children simply do not show the type of imaginative development with which the professionals are familiar; their imagination has been applied to survival in the streets.

Should we teach make-believe play? We have pointed out that imagination is everywhere, although the modern forms of make-believe are of one type only and that type is very extensive. A number of modern investigators have tried, fairly successfully, to teach modern kinds of make-believe to poverty children. They have been able to show that teaching make-believe improves make-believe play and also that children who have gone through quite a short program of make-believe teaching also improve their scores in creativity tests. (In creativity tests one gets a high score for having original or unusual ideas about how to use different objects, words, or diagrams.)

Children of the future, who are more likely to work with computers and must understand automation, may need a lot more make-believe play than they are currently being taught. In make-believe, as in most modern work, one deals with *symbols* rather than *things*. Make-believe play is symbolic play. Children play with representations of things rather than with the things themselves, and that is what so much of the modern world is like. We manage our lives with words, pictures, or numbers, all of which are symbols.

As with all game playing, the make-believe that is introduced should be made consistent with the current make-believe of your children. Sometimes three-year-olds who are being judged not to indulge in make-believe can be seen doing quite a bit of it on the jungle gym or while chasing in and out of the swings. Often these high moments of social interaction are overlooked by many teachers because they are rowdy and boisterous. Yet surely a first step might be to encourage these higher moments of interaction and to add to *their* symbolism.

Why not give the chasers some monster costumes to wear? Have a safe base that is painted like an apartment. Gradually develop rules for being safe on white sidewalk lines painted on the playground but not safe off these lines. This, of course, requires teacher or parent participation; they must give examples of how to play. They have to set limits and insist on turn-taking. Perhaps in the beginning tagging will not be essential. A player who is being chased should walk innocently until the monster emerges and then run for the safe base, always arriving safely. The monster's job is merely to threaten and to chase, but events can be so arranged that the monster never catches the player.

Many more examples can be developed of make-believe extensions of the highest level of social play that the children have already reached. This seems a natural way to proceed but has seldom been followed, perhaps because we as parents and teachers are not used to applying our imagination to the development of children who imagine in other ways.

The most important principle in all this is that you *teach this kind of play by playing.* You do not talk about it. You do not say "What do you want to play?" or "What shall we do now?" That is fatal. You act out playing with a doll yourself, being its mother, or you play the doctor examining the baby in make-believe. Are we talking about make-believe too early here? No; make-believe can be in the child's own behavior as early as three years of age. If we do not assist at this point, it gets harder as the years go by. All of our current research would also suggest that we will have a greater long-term effect on children if we teach their *parents* how to engage in the make-believe with their own children. Teaching children is not as effective as teaching parents.

THE CHILD'S OWN PLAY

Social Play

One of our problems in writing about children's social play is that traditionally children as young as two or three years old have not been studied extensively. Thus, when we say that four-year-olds can do something, it may well turn out that as there is more opportunity for children to be together in the earlier years, even two-year-olds will be able to do these things. For that we must wait and see. The point of this part of the chapter is that just as you can observe children's levels of solitary play, you can also observe their levels of social play.

Between the ages of two and four years it becomes increasingly difficult to tell the difference between solitary and social play because there is a mixture of both. In the nursery situation or in your own home individual children play at their own things but quite often watch others, imitate something the others are doing, share something with someone else, and very occasionally participate in somebody else's play idea. A few moments of shared play may be sufficient for the announcement that they have a "friend."

As we have said earlier, most people, including children, spend most of their free time watching others. Football and baseball were not the earliest spectator sports. In the nursery school or anywhere else where there are other children about, they attract each other's attention. If one child is doing something that can be copied, another child may soon be doing the same thing. If one is piling blocks on top of each other, another will probably soon be doing so. This is *contagion play*.

Occasionally as children imitate each other, they accidentally do the same thing together. One child is banging a block, another does the same, another does the same, and in no time a table full of three-year-olds are busy thumping more or less in time. The teacher comes running in great annoyance, but at that moment the three-year-olds have reached a very high peak of social existence for them. This can be called *unison play*.

When we realize that rhythm, group prayer, ritual, and choral activity have played a leading role in every society that we know of, it becomes clear that the children's discovery is one that is universal with mankind. It is not cynical to say that in some ways unison activity is the highest social peak of which people are capable. It is the only time when they are truly *at one* with each other in a way that provides evidence of everyone's involvement.

Anyway, this is what three-year-olds discover and what intelligent teachers of three-year-olds use in their rhythm and movement classes, with simple songs or the beating of a drum. At this age children rise to a new peak when they are helped to sing along or move along at the same time with others.

At three also, with a little bit of pressure from the teachers and later from each other, they can manage social behavior if they take turns. *Turn-taking*, which is being studied by Dr. Catherine Garvey, of Johns Hopkins University, is one of those universals of human behavior that facilitate all sorts of social activities (from concert performances to getting on buses). There are several levels within this that deserve mention:

1. We take turns, but we do the same thing. We echo each other. One child bangs her block twice, the next

child bangs his block twice, the first bangs hers again twice, the second bangs his again twice. Thus, we have alternation of the same behavior.

2. We take turns, but we do different things that we repeat. One child makes the sounds of a lion, the other responds by making the sounds of a bear; the first repeats the lion, the second the bear.

3. We take turns, but we change as we go. One child is a lion, the next a tiger; then the first is a gorilla, the second a dog; the first is a cow, the second a cat; etc. Most conversations in early childhood are like this.

Obviously more-complex forms would be involved if more children participated, as they will in the succeeding years. At this point managing two together is a significant accomplishment.

The easiest form of play for a child is where everyone does what he wants them to, and that is the basic form of organization in authoritarian societies. It is the most natural thing in the world for three-year-olds to want to be the center pin of any play activity. Their capacity for insight into the feelings or behaviors of others is as yet very limited. A great deal of young children's play during this and the next four years will be structured around one dominant player—that is, *central-person play*.

You might ask how the other children put up with it. They are also egocentric. They also want the play structured around them. Although that is true, even more important for young children is to be included in play with others. So if a dominant child actually has ideas for play and can tell the others what to do, which takes a fair bit of precocity at three years but will be more common by five years, others will often willingly join in, because the maintenance of social play, the being with others, hardly otherwise occurs.

It is important to stress how fundamental this kind of play is. Most of the games children will play up to ten years of age center on the actions of a central person. All the chasing games, all the circle games, focus on the player who is "It" and what that player does. So central-person play is not just egocentricity; it is the mutual fitting together of the dominance of one child and the dependence of the others.

So strong is such central-person play that occasionally in later years a particularly strong leader child will lead a whole group of peers off into some wild escapade, even of potential danger, such as stone throwing, running across the road, pursuing some other frightened children, etc. But this is more typical of four- and five-year-olds than of three-year-olds. It is the first form of charismatic leadership.

Occasionally at this age a group of children will be welded together by their real or fantasied fear of some dangerous central figure, such as a dog or a monster, and they will all run squealing into some place of retreat. This is a unison activity in its way. It is usually very temporary, because most of the children cannot manage the potentially real quality of the fear. They are not quite brave enough to play this yet, unless the feared person or thing is really thoroughly familiar and reassuring.

Sometimes even at this age children are able to aggregate together in a loose form of play association around a *common theme*. Most often this has to do with houses and families, which are the most familiar common theme for all the players. Another common theme is going to the supermarket. At this stage each player's imaginings are different from the others'. But the objects, the words, and some of the processes are similar, so there is considerable parallelism within the same space. They occasionally exchange and go through cooperative processes (handing over goods), but this is ritual rather than insight.

As before, however, the presence of a slightly older child will support many of these common themes. Thus, one will be the witch, and the other runs away, each taking turns in frightening the other in a chase up the stairs; or one is the fireman and wakes the other up out of bed, and they both run from the fire; or one is the teacher and the other the pupil; or one the doctor and the other the patient; or one the store-keeper and the other the buyer. In each of these only one or two simple interactions occur. They run away from the witch; they run together from the fire; the teacher spanks the pupil; the doctor gives a shot to the patient, who goes to sleep; the storekeeper gives articles to the buyer, who takes them away.

Although children of three can seldom do these things with age peers, they can participate quite well in these fairly one-sided exchanges with older children. In fact their reaction may help to guide the older child, but their reaction may also be irrelevant to the general plot. Still, there is a reciprocation of sorts that does move the younger player closer to true sharing.

Social life is half cooperation and half bossiness. We have been discussing how three-year-olds get it together; now we shall take up the question of how they decide who is boss, which is a form of social testing. The business of central-person play shows that often they get together by agreeing that someone is in charge. There is little verbal agreement in this, and the person in charge may have only temporary status. All that child may do is be the one that starts something. After that it is follow the leader for a little while. A good example of this is a group of three-year-olds eating lunch outdoors. One of them starts to roll down the grassy bank. Soon all are rolling down the grassy bank and copying what any other innovative child newly introduces.

But this kind of thing is not an accident. In any free nursery school situation there is an incessant vying for power. Individual children try to influence others to do what they want to have done. Children vary greatly in doing this by temperament and by prior experience. Some try incessantly to influence others, while others do not. These efforts are not simply a clash of egocentric wills. Much of it has to do with social and play management. You cannot play together unless there is some consensus, and that consensus has to be worked out.

The management of play is a difficult problem, and up until about the age of ten or so children may spend just as much time in arguing about management as they will in playing. This is the reason why many psychologists feel that free play is so valuable for children. They really do have to work out the rules for creating social life in their play. These cannot just be given to them by telling them to be cooperative. Sometimes a parent can discreetly support the authority of individual children so they can organize the others for a little longer.

In a study of our own we found that children even at the age of three use a wide diversity of power tactics with each other. They use physical means, they use verbal means, and they use strategies. Sometimes they just cry for help. They scream, put out their hands, plead, ask, pretend to cry, or offer gifts. They threaten to exclude others or offer to let them into the group. They try to get in by smiling, bribing, requesting, reasoning, distracting other children, or making someone else the target.

We found that girls more often used the technique of threatening exclusion than did three-year-old boys. Boys more often used physical attack and also verbal and strategic attack. (An example of strategic attack is creating a fantasy of what will happen to the other child if that child does not oblige. "If you don't give me that, the teacher will shut you in the closet.") Boys also use more straight bossy behavior. In fact, the three-year-old boys in our group used more power tactics than did the girls. This was surprising because these were children of professionals where the mother and the father both worked and the children had few other differences in their kinds of play.

Our feeling is that although it is possible to discover many differences between boys and girls in their play, there is little that is inevitable about any of these. Each sex can learn the play and the games that the other sex does. Individual differences are always more pronounced than are group sex differences, even though in the history of human culture the division of work between the sexes has apparently been a good survival technique. Other research also shows that although boys and girls do not differ greatly in the amount of activity that they show in play, boys get much more active when they are around other boys. It seems that in some way parents give to boys the notion that it is their job to struggle and to be concerned with power relationships with other boys.

These present sex differences are in accord with the general finding that boys are more aggressive in play and in other behavior at all ages. The parents of boys would not argue with that. The differences are not only in physical aggression. The aggressiveness hides a variety of more-subtle influence attempts that have to do primarily with establishing one's place among a group of other children. An animal psychologist, for example, might argue that males are more concerned with pecking orders and their place in them than are females and that this is reflected in the play activities of both animals and children. It seems that in school playgrounds, as well as in more-informal situations, boys are much more concerned than are girls with their power relationships. These power relationships are not well sorted out until about seven years of age, when pecking orders take on a fairly stable form. Girls, on the other hand, tend to be more concerned with power relationships in small groups of one or two friends. Including and excluding are power tactics for the family or for friends. Perhaps these differences will change as time passes. At present they are still strong.

Solitary Play

It is becoming harder to separate progress in social play from progress in solitary play, and these lines will begin to break down in this chapter. Exploration and testing will concern us less from now on, partly because we are dealing predominantly with the urban world. For better or for worse, those who have written about children's play have not had very much to say about rural children or poor children, who still carry on many very serious encounters with a difficult and dangerous environment.

If we can assume that more and more children will gradually learn to play like children of comfortable means, then this chapter has value for the future. If, however, we decide in some novel way to turn our children back into some more-challenging physical environment, new books on play will be necessary. This may be the way we will go, in view of our current interest in ecology. Perhaps we need a series of playgrounds changing in scope from small-scale adventures with climbing and building possibilities to increasingly larger natural territories for exploration, going all the way up to mountain ranges for late adolescents. The latter group is better catered to, with scouts and searchers doing pretty much what we advocate.

The most interesting development that becomes obvious in three- and four-year-olds is verbal and intellectual *exploration*. In a sense these intellectual forms of mastery become more obvious, since the older physical forms now extend into much larger territorial concerns, such as making visits and exploring alleyways.

Their ability with small motor skills means that many conventional (Montessori) types of toys or apparatus will keep children busy for a long time. Sorting and matching games and jigsaw puzzles of increasing complexity become more challenging. They become more interested in hammer and nail sets, sorting boxes, buttoning books, paper cutting, and design matching. At the same time they are more interested in visits and excursions; exploring new playgrounds; learning about plants, trees, and animals; and even growing things. Children like to assist in being gardeners.

Their intellectual exploration is endless. They want to know why but end up coupling things together without understanding, as in the example at the beginning of this chapter: "I have a cut on my eye. That's why I fell over." Children find it difficult to disentangle cause and effect. Two things are known to be linked, and the word "cause," which is associated with linkage, is used, often with amusing reversals.

> "I love you Daddy."
> "Why?"
> "Cause you went in an airplane yesterday and you brought me a present. A doll."

Coming home in the airplane is confused with going, but she puts together the bringing of the present and the love she feels.

Some other examples follow in which relationships are explored but not always put in the "logic" of adults:

> If you get mad at me, I won't come to Christmas.

> What's that thing you've got hanging off your peewee?

"I'm a person from the city."
"Why?"
"Cause I bring things."

Little children cannot be made to go to bed.

When it's warm, it's warm, and then we can go out to winter.

"What will you be when you grow up?"
"I'll be a twin. I'm going to be a Cinderella with long hair down to my sleeves."

I haven't had a bath cause my dirty legs are here. [pointing]

"Why are you a girl?"
"Cause I eat poisoned apples." [after hearing "Snow White"]

You're nice 'cause I like you.

The important step in children's *imitative play* is that they really begin to put some personality into their characters. Up until this year children have played the roles fairly straight; that is, they have been a mother or a father carrying out everyday actions like dressing and washing. Now, however, they begin to play an "angry" father or a "naughty" child. In this third year they really begin to get some feeling into their make-believe people.

In addition, they can now run a small society with their truck drivers or dolls, with several people being represented by toy figures. They may even occasionally use different "voices" when speaking the parts for these characters. This is another aspect of the personality differences that they now attribute to people. Most of the characters played are adults or other powerful people. Although babies are used to vent childish feelings, the general tendency is to play out the roles of the powerful people that the child would like to be.

In addition to exploration, testing, and imitation, we notice *construction* now. It is our fourth type of mastery and is to be found in children's organization of their personal space in their bedrooms and in their attempts to make a building out of wood or boxes outdoors. Since they cannot master the adult world, most construction happens in their play world. First they learn to handle their toys, then they start to construct things with them. Toys become worlds of their own.

Play construction borrows from play exploration, testing, and imitation, but particularly from imitation. The word "construction" is used to refer to things that are made and constructed with objects (small houses, forts, cities, etc.) through which children can imitate adults by manipulating things. In imitative play there is a more direct imitation through playing roles.

When our own children were of this age, they would always take one of their constructed worlds into any new environment. Their major worlds were those of houses and stores. Whenever we went away for the summer, stayed in another house, or even simply went to the beach for a day, this group of two-, four-, six-, and eight-year-olds would immediately set up their space in the new environment. Different families or groups of children within a family tend to have a game that travels with them. For some they are always competitive; others have traveling intellectual contests (particularly while riding in their car); and yet others transfer constructed worlds, as ours did.

In general at this age children's imaginative play is helped by having such miniature toy worlds to play with. If children are not particularly imaginative, such toys help. For children who are already very imaginative, toys are not quite so necessary; they can make their own toys out of anything. Thus, it is important to know which children we are talking about before we praise or condemn giving them toys to play with.

Within moderation we feel it is wise for all children to have some toys. One of the unfortunate things in our society is that those who have the most fantasy and need manufactured toys the least are the ones who have the most. But where poverty stalks, there is also poverty of imagination. There is a tendency for the poor to buy toys that are momentary, mechanical gimmicks rather than long-serving toys, such as miniature cars, blocks, tea sets, and doll sets, that provide a way of thinking imaginatively. Although, as we said earlier, they do not provide such a way if you have not learned how to use them imaginatively, and you learn that best from your parents.

8 | Primitive Society— Order and Disorder:

From Four to Five Years

"Who are you going to marry?" she asks.
"My father," says the boy.
"You can't marry him."
"Yes I can; he goes to work."

●

"Where do people come from?"
"From seeds."
"Do they have pictures of people on the packets?"

●

"Little girls are made of spice and all things nice," says her mother.
"They are not, they're made of skin," answers the daughter.

Children are able to create different types of *order* in the years from four to five. They have an enormous need to discover ways of getting along successfully with other children as they branch out from their homes and become independent in kindergartens and playgrounds. If they do not, their own egocentricity will ruin all efforts at playing with others. They become almost desperately concerned with being able to play with others. Thus, our own play with them (in a group), as well as their play with each other, usually has to be very ritualistic and orderly.

As children come increasingly into touch with the world, they have to know how to behave in public. They have to learn etiquette. They must learn not to pick their noses, spit, or soil their underwear. They must learn how to wait their turn, not to stare, and not to yell. It is not surprising, therefore, that they often feel powerless and overwhelmed or dream of being helpless victims in the face of monstrous creatures. They avidly begin their diet of fairy tales, cartoons, and stories, which help to convince them that success and victory are possible—an addiction from which they will not recover, if they ever do, until around twelve years of age.

Simultaneously, children try to understand everything that is happening about them. Their philosophies and rule systems have the flavor of the anecdotes above. They have rules for girls and for boys, for where babies come from, and for anything else that comes their way. Although they have reached an age for making rules, they do not yet have the logical grasp to make them consistent. Their rules are made on the basis of their own particular experiences and without adequate knowledge of all the issues involved.

While this struggling for order is going on in their heads

and in their social lives, you can become more and more flexible on the home front. By four years you and your children have ironed out a great deal. They know your routines and requirements, and you have a pretty good idea of their needs and limitations. This order, which is already well established, can give you both a great deal of freedom. For this reason the first part of this chapter can be about much more versatile regimes than can the later parts in which we must deal with children's struggle for order in their new child society.

GAMES AND OTHER THINGS TO DO

Coaching and Controlling Make-Believe

Let us assume that by now we have stimulated the children's powers of make-believe. The problem for most parents now is that they feel they should control make-believe rather than stimulate it. Traditionally, people feel that there is something wrong about imagination. People who have mainly valued physical forms of mastery often have felt that their children were too fanciful and perhaps even mentally a little astray, with imaginary companions and the like; thus, their tendency has been to encourage work habits rather than fancy. There is little to worry about in children's fantasy, however, unless they keep on make-believing the same theme or situation, in which case they may be demonstrating that they are trying to free themselves from some fixed and unpleasant circumstance. Even here the problem lies with what is worrying them, not with their attempts to master their worries.

Many parents worry about other aspects of children's fantasy between four and seven years of age. In particular, they are concerned with the presence of violence and the use of guns. In many kindergartens guns and aggressive play are completely forbidden. Perhaps we must ask ourselves whether it makes sense to take guns away from children who grow up seeing these things constantly represented on television and in movies. We live in a country where those who manufacture and sell guns are of such great political power that it is impossible to enact legislation against their sale, although most police forces would prefer to see guns banned entirely. The question therefore boils down to whether it makes sense to stop children's trying to manage the violence that constantly assails them if we do not ourselves control those who spread such violence.

So we have a dilemma: It makes sense not to allow children to play at war as one small step toward a more peaceful world, but it does not make sense to believe this if we do not change the world in which they live, for otherwise that first small step will not make any difference. Furthermore, children have to cope with these warlike influences themselves, and they are not helped merely by being told that they must not play with guns.

In these hopeless circumstances we think that you should not ban war play altogether (if some children want it), but you should instead insist that the children play in a make-believe way. There should be no toy guns, only pretend guns —with their fingers, so no one gets hurt—and all deaths are symbolic. We are distinguishing between pretend shooting and physically grabbing each other, holding down, and roughing up, maybe hurting.

One of the most effective forms of dramatization with four- to seven-year-olds—in fact, with children of any elementary school age—is the improvisation of dying a violent death. The argument here is that the stress on make-believe (rather than toy facsimilization) heightens children's symbolic control of their feelings and their warlike games are less likely to break down into direct aggression. It is noticeable even at three years of age that those children who can imagine ray guns and space attacks have less difficulty in relating to each other than do those who have no such symbols for their aggressive feelings.

This has been advice for those who manage children in large groups and who do not have much time to participate individually in children's make-believe play. For parents who play with their own children or with smaller groups and therefore have more time we believe more-advanced steps can be taken. We think that where there is adequate help, you can encourage games of space adventure and seafaring adventures, as well as exploring activities in real woods and at the beach. What children of this age must feel in their make-believe, exploratory, and testing activities is fantasied *courage and adequacy*. War play is one of the most obvious ways in which this is expressed. There are many others, and you can foster these by stories, dramatic play, and joining in with your children. We must not take away the fantasy of courage at this age; thus, if we do take away war play, then we must look for other ways to encourage its development.

Group Pantomime

Between the ages of four and seven children usually become very self-conscious about being on stage. Since the age of one year and thereafter they have developed exhibitionistic behavior within the circle of the willing family. They perform, and their parents applaud. But because they want to be accepted by other children at this age and yet still hang on to their desire for being the center of attention, which was allowed in the family, they are mightily embarrassed to be out there performing in front of other children.

It is not surprising that most of their first games allow for such central roles in an acceptable turn-taking way. The games allow them to hide their desire to be out in front behind the ritual moves of the game. Punchinello is the funny fellow that we watch in the game of the same name where children take turns at making movements in the middle of the circle. There is quite a poetic literature of reminiscences about taking such roles in the center of ring games. Some children love them. Others cannot stand the embarrassment of suddenly becoming the center of attention.

Although four- to seven-year-olds are capable of make-believe dramatic play when they are with other children, often if they are asked to stand up on stage and make believe, they will not do it. Parents and teachers should emphasize ring games like Punchinello or use group unison rhythmic and imitative games. We all act at being hopping rabbits at the same time, or we are all crowing roosters, or we are all growling lions prowling about the floor and then suddenly running from the elephant.

Once more, as parents we must get over our own embarrassments and use our own imaginations in acting out the central person. This provides a cover for the role playing of everyone else. As any kindergarten teacher knows, it takes a dramatic and convincing performance to keep an entire group going. Not all adults have the necessary physical mobility and dramatic conviction to elicit a continuous performance from a large class of four-year-olds. Still, most parents can mimic an animal with smaller groups of half a dozen children and with their own children. This is one of the great games to play at this age—mother and child or teacher and children mimicking animals together. The children can improvise and perhaps be a star without feeling that someone is watching them. Usually in school some children eagerly volunteer to take turns at being leader in this follow-the-leader type of activity, which is a break for the teacher.

Puppets

Hand puppets, brown bag puppets, or even dolls can be used to serve the same kind of objectifying purpose for these exhibitionistic feelings. The group was a mask for the child's sensitive self. Now the puppet becomes the mask. First use the puppet to talk about household activities and the sort of content you have seen in the children's own play. Follow the children's lead. Two-person dialogues are easiest to begin with. Enjoy the fact that the children can find their voice (perhaps a high squeaky one) through the puppet when they would not dare put on the same voice directly as an "actor" in front of the class. It is easier to act first through the toy objects or puppets, then through the roles of other people very different from ourselves, and only finally through people like ourselves. Not many children can "act" like themselves.

Sometimes puppets can be started through toy telephone conversations, which makes a good game even without puppets. Perhaps because we do not see the other person and that person cannot see us, telephones make us less self-conscious and permit various voices to be tried out. We can even sit back-to-back to heighten our protection. It is an interesting psychological interpretation that in acting before audiences we mainly fear ourselves rather than the audience. By acting as a group, by puppets, by telephones, by masks, or by makeup we can forget that self and be whatever it is we want to be.

Four-year-olds have great problems when they have to sort out (*a*) being a central person, looked at and admired by all in the family; (*b*) being a self, expected to be responsible and sane at nursery school; and (*c*) acting a role for others to see, as a puppet or an actor. These are not easy discriminations to make, and they will not be clearly sorted out until about the age of seven.

Puppetry at this age is generally in terms of fairly conventional dialogues between two and occasionally three players. With experience your children can introduce imaginary characters.

Story Reversals

Many of your stories have now become rituals; that is, they have been told fairly conventionally for a year or two. Just as we have misnamed pictures and made foolish mistakes in simple picture books in earlier years, we now can move into story idiocy. Begin, for example, by announcing the story of "The Two Little Pigs and the Big Bad Bull," "Goldilocks and the Two Bears," or "Cinderella and the Four Ugly Blisters." On the child's reprimand confess your mistake, then make another.

For some children this is no good. It may be too upsetting; it is not fun; in which case content yourself with playing it straight. Remember that even playing it straight can be good fun with adequate dramatization. The father bear can always make deeper grunts. The frog prince can have a superlative croak. You should have been developing your animal sounds over the past few years and also your range of witchly and princessly voices. There is a lot of fun and drama in that prop box, and both you and your young audience can enjoy it.

Still, if you are allowed, the time has come to break loose from merely good impersonations. A few blunders can be followed by a completely wacky nursery tale, always submitting to the child's corrections and making apologies as you proceed. Again, if your children are "playful," they will let you develop completely new tales out of the old ones. The possibilities here are endless. James Thurber had some versions of his own that you might consult (*Fables For Our Time* and *Further Fables For Our Time*). Basically you have small creatures (pups, children) who suffer some misfortune at the hands of evil characters (witches, wolves) and go into hiding or some period of suffering (Cinderella as a maid, Snow White into hiding) and then come into their own as a result of magic, fortunate circumstance, or trickery (a fairy queen, a prince, the tricky third pig).

You can see how successful you are in due course by your child's own participation. What you ultimately want is a wacky story that the two of you construct together.

On Being a Play Mimic

Research evidence suggests that most adults, when talking to children, do so in simpler sentences than they use for other adults. Even slightly older children talk more simply to younger children. Yet very few people are aware of doing so. Like parents who do "ootchy cootchy" with their six-month-old babies, these are systematic forms of behavior of which we are not very conscious. We may not admit this because we would be embarrassed to acknowledge it, just as we are embarrassed by other adults who use baby talk, so this presents something of a problem.

How are we to get you way beyond even simple sentences into frog croaks, dogs' barking, and pigs' grunting without your feeling a loss of your dignity? Perhaps we should sing a few rounds of "Old MacDonald Had a Farm" for warm-up. What we hope is that after you have followed the diet of games throughout the last few chapters, making animal noises will be nothing to you now. You will have worked your way through animal picture books with sounds and imitations. You will have led or followed your three-year-old around the carpet puffing like a railway train. You will now also be a regular James Thurber, making up nonsense nursery tales accompanied by the magic of sound effects and impersonations.

Celebrations

There is a whole category of activities with your child that we have not included yet because they do not really come under the heading of games or play. We will call them celebrations. All young parents remember the first Christmas with their firstborn. He stands there unsteadily, transfixed by the tree. He grabs for everything—the glass ornaments, the candles, the candies; he gets hysterical with all the wrapping paper. You look indulgently at him and say to each other, "Next Christmas will be his first *real* Christmas."

That is just the beginning. The American calendar is like the old movie *Holiday Inn*. There is a festival every month, and by the time children are in kindergarten they seem to celebrate them all: Valentine's Day, Easter, May Day, July 4th, and Halloween. Those are just the national celebrations. In addition, there are family birthdays, bar and bas mitzvahs, first communions, "flying ups," graduations, and more. The initial impetus to observe all these occasions usually comes from the parent or the teacher, but by the time they are established in your family's way of life everyone generally plays an important role.

These occasions provide ritual, family cohesiveness, and affection that children remember with nostalgia all through their growing-up period. Because food plays a major role here, the mother or father has the opportunity to teach the child how to cook. It is usually fun food, such as cupcakes for birthdays and Valentine's Day, Christmas cookies, and decorated Easter eggs. Boys as well as girls should have the opportunity to feel comfortable in the kitchen. It is fun for everyone. It becomes a game, a challenge of sorts, for a six-year-old to spread out six dozen baked cookies and frost and decorate them.

Then there are homemade decorations. A family with young children is always running out of construction paper. All the homemade birthday cards, welcome-home signs after business trips, and potato-cut Christmas cards demand a respect for, and appreciation of, each other's artistic talents. In this category would come pie making. Children can make their own "pie" out of scraps of dough that you give them while you are making pies. They can also hammer on scraps of wood while you are doing some carpentry. Today, fathers are as likely to be in the kitchen as mothers are to be hammering—an admirable turn of events.

When children are sick, they will need all the quiet but entertaining activities you have been sharing with them— this in addition to eight hours of TV a day. From the time children have reached the age of three you will have been cutting out paper dolls and animals for them. It is a short step for them to learn to make clothes with real material for their dolls. Although even in this emancipated age not too many boys would make doll's clothes, all children can learn to knit, crochet, or do macramé. From making their own greeting cards they progress to writing their own poetry and stories. They do this in school anyway. Given the proper appreciation, they soon learn that their own literary efforts, especially if they learn to make illustrated cardboard covers to preserve them like "real" books, make a most acceptable gift. Some of our most prized possessions are the books of haiku or stories our children secretly made for us.

We should emphasize once again that it is better to face the fact that a creative childhood is going to be messy. To have that nice thin firm cardboard available that your children are always asking for means that the top of your refrigerator will be permanently piled with empty cornflake or saltine boxes. To keep sick children happy you will have to establish them regally in the living room, not in their isolated bedroom, with all the snacks, craft supplies, and comic books strewn around them. If the Avon lady comes, do not apologize.

Group Games with Children

Up until this chapter we have been pretty much treating the reader as an individual parent relating to one child. The examples in the last chapter of children's group play, the power tactics used by them, and their make-believe extend our interest to the nursery school type of group as well.

With this chapter the adult we have in mind is as much a teacher or nursery school worker as an individual parent. We begin this new emphasis with a critical account of *games of order and disorder*. By this we mean the old circle or ring games. There are some who feel that these activities are no longer important to young children. They have faded from the children's own group play traditions in many suburban areas, and there is a feeling consequently that they are out of date. We think we should be careful about jumping too quickly to that conclusion.

In brief, our argument will be that games and activities in which the players act in unison and in a cooperative way, such as singing, dancing, and being rhythmic together, are one of the very important ways in which four- to seven-year-olds gain a sense of social togetherness. In some nursery schools and homes the adult is skillful in singing catchy songs and in conducting rhythmic movements to drums and the like; in these cases the need is well satisfied in a very "modern" way. But for most of us who lack the skills to invent our own rhythms for the occasion, traditional forms of expression are a most useful and valuable way in which we can play games with children.

The most basic games in early childhood, and in all cultures of the world, have to do with the acting out of order and disorder. The most important thing that human groups have to learn socially is how to collaborate together, and that means they must learn how to deal with the forces of anarchy and chaos that are always present. In young children the chaos is often produced by their own incompetence. In adults, as we all know, divisiveness is always present.

The games we deal with here sometimes emphasize mainly order, sometimes mainly disorder, sometimes a mixture of both. But either way, they all mirror, model, or state the conflict that constantly underlies the social contract that keeps us together. Your attitude should be to try to discover what new fun you can have with these games. The adult who acts only as the group leader or educator and does not participate is less likely to enjoy what is going on and less likely to help the children through this kind of play.

The most obvious game of this kind is "Ring around the Rosy," where all the children dance round in a circle holding hands in an orderly way until the last two lines—"Ashes, ashes [or "One, two, three, four"],/We all fall down"— whereupon everyone collapses on the ground. There is another game where all the players hold hands like a long string and wind around each other until they are a tight ball. Then they run it out until it breaks, and they all fall down or apart.

In another game, which comes from Melanesia, the children all squat in a row on their heels and pass their hands between their legs. They clasp the backs of their left legs with their left hands, and their right legs with their right hands. Then they chant a song about the "kiwiwi" bird that has an ending of "pip, pip, pip," during which the children try to jump backward. Some children always fall over, and there is much laughter among the players and those watching.

Other games in which orderliness is emphasized are "Here We Go Round the Mulberry Bush," "Punchinello," and "The Farmer in the Dell" (although there is usually roughhousing when all the children pick the poor cheese). "London Bridge" breaks down into disorder with the tug of war at the end. These later games, sometimes called ring games, singing games, or ritual dramas, are usually an orderly statement of childish wishes. In European culture most of these games center on the conflict of females over acceptance and rejection. The players, who are powerless children, are pretending to be powerful adults. In life these children have no say yet in love and marriage, although in the game they do. The farmer gets to choose a wife. Punchinello is a "star."

Children find it hard to play these games to keep time as they march and sing. It is evident that part of the function of the games is to overcome their own childish lack of organization. It is an accomplishment for five- to seven-year-olds to get through them without the games' falling apart, because some children cannot do what is required. At this age then, a game of order is mastery over incompetence, not only mastery over love and marriage. These order-disorder games are not unlike the previous games that three-year-olds played, such as building sand castles and knocking them down.

In addition, there are games of direct disorder. Children, as well as adults, get great pleasure from whirling and whirling until they collapse with dizziness, from rolling down slopes, from twirling around on an icy pond, from swinging, sliding, and tobogganing. They can now ignore the very things they were trying to control in the previous games.

We have talked at length about these games just to illustrate how important they are. Even "Ring around the Rosy" is part of a larger system of social learning. When we play games like this with children, they are not casual happenings. Every game is an illustration of some system of social relationships. Our theory is that children can deal with this social system better in the game situation than in their everyday affairs.

THE CHILD'S OWN PLAY

Social Play

The games of order and disorder we have just described show one of the ways in which human groups have attempted to solve the problem of social cohesion versus social chaos. All the tactics introduced in the last chapter are used repeatedly by four-year-olds but without much insight. Three-year-olds are even cruder when they use these tactics. Between the ages of four and seven, however, children begin to shape up their pecking orders so that these are fairly well established by the age of seven.

To do this they continue the unison, contagion, turn-taking, and central-person play that we described in the last chapter. In addition, they get better in the following social forms: common fantasies, story play, and group customs.

Stereotyped ideas hold adults together. The same is true for young children. Their most common ideas have to do with houses and forms of travel, usually in cars. *Play fantasies* that have to do with the house theme now become a basis for their social play. Earlier and more elementary games, like solitary house play, turn into more elaborate games of house with other children. Because they can take for granted such sequences as cooking, eating, washing, and going to bed or gassing up, driving, carrying, and garaging, four-year-olds are more able to deal with the problem of who gets to be the cook and who gets to drive the truck, which is harder for them.

Apparently, the more powerful and authoritarian the parents, the more rigidly the children act out the routines of adult daily life in their play. When their parents pressure them to conform, their play must deal with that conflict, and they do so by reproducing exactly in their play how their parents behave. In this way they, in their own right, try to be powerful in the miniature play world.

It is widely supposed that *television* and movies provide children today with many more common themes for group play than children used to have. This may well be true. We have seen three-year-olds acting out a television weather session. One child spoke through a cardboard frame about tomorrow's weather, while two others sitting in a seat talked about having to wear coats and other accessories. There are also reports, however, of children who watch lots of television being less social than children used to be. Probably what this means is that television does not help unless you are already engaged in a great deal of social play and are learning ways of introducing television material into play content. We repeat once again, you or your children's teachers may have to participate in their games to show them how this is done.

Unfortunately, one way children get together in kindergarten is on the basis of *sex*. We watched a trio of four-year-old girls in a kindergarten setting. They decided to "build a house" using all the large blocks "before the boys come." As each boy entered, their play was reinforced as they announced, "You can't come in. You're a boy, and this is for girls," even though none of the boys made any attempt to enter.

Another way for four-year-olds to get together is by *ritual*. We mentioned earlier the rituallike games of order and disorder. But informal groups also tend to establish rituals if they play together for any period of time, although perhaps the term *group habits* is more appropriate here since there is no tradition to these customs. What tends to happen is that a group decides such things as who should sit where, who plays with what, which objects are to be played with privately and which are common objects for the group as a whole, what the sequence of games will be, what words they will use to refer to their activities, and who shall be in charge of which territories.

From the age of four onward, when children have time for free play and are largely not interfered with, they work out agreements of this sort in their play groups. Also, when such a group is well established, research evidence shows that it is very hard for new players, even powerful ones, to disrupt these group habits. Usually new players cannot influence the others until they accept and go along with the group's customs. All this is most interesting because it shows that at the same time as four- to seven-year-olds are being forced to conform to public etiquette in the outside society, they are also creating their own simple forms for controlling their own play groups.

Inclusion and *exclusion* are powerful forces at this age. Nothing holds people together like enemies, and friends and enemies become quite an important part of social play during these years. Real or imagined, other enemies will sometimes keep a small group of two or more children together in some cosy place of their own. As long as the enemies are imagined, there is no harm in this. But the relief from their inability to control love and hate that comes when the group discovers an outside menace is unfortunately often too strong to allow to go unchecked. Sometimes four-year-olds foster their group life by scapegoating, disliking, and jeering at some poor innocent person that happens by or has some easily identified negative characteristic.

Children vary greatly in the skills that they bring to getting into a group with other children. The most successful technique seems to be simply to engage in play that is relevant to what is going on. "Look, I'm a jet airplane." This seems to work better than "Can I play?" The principle of doing something playful instead of asking to be included apparently works as well for children as it works for adults who want to join in children's play. But smiles, giggles, crying, stunts, ludicrous expressions, and mock attacks are among the equipment that children use.

A group formation usually consists of two or, at most, three children, and a persistent child can usually get in. Sometimes children who are told that they cannot play just sit nearby. Later they ask, "Can I watch?" After a while they discover some low-level and useful role. "Can I be the baby?" "Yes." Then when they are in, they can work up to higher roles. "Now it's my turn to be the mother." Clearly it would be of great value if we knew more about successful social-entry techniques and how these might be demonstrated to children who have difficulty gaining entry.

Solitary Play

The *exploratory* and *testing* games begin to disappear as we move up the age span because children now tend to enjoy indoor activities, such as building, painting, crayoning, printing, pasting, clay modeling, sewing, sorting, dressing up, puppets, cooking, music, plants, animals, tools, and hardware. If we go off exploring with adults at age four, it is often on a visit to the fire station, the wharf, the ferry, the zoo, the printer's, a nature hike, the post office, the pet shop, or the library.

This does not mean, of course, that children at this age do not explore and test in their own backyards and nearby parks, hills, or trees. These activities are simply not a major way of life as they were in earlier times and still are for non-urban or suburbanized children. Four- to seven-year-olds will still run a lot, hop, jump, gallop and so on. By five years of age most children can hop on one foot for fifty feet in about ten seconds. Most five-year-olds cannot skip yet; they tend to skip on one foot and walk on the other. But they can run at about twelve feet per second, and they can jump about three feet.

Most five-year-olds can also stand on one foot for several seconds or can walk around a circular white line without falling off. By this age too they can walk with alternating feet along a balance beam lying on the floor. They begin to be able to catch an eight-inch ball with their elbows at their sides rather than with their arms stretched out in front. About half the children at this age can bounce a tennis ball with both hands and catch it with both hands, and most can catch a large playground ball bounced to them.

These various norms give us some idea of the mastery practice and, by implication, the play that has been going on in physical areas between four and five years of age.

Construction and *imitative play* and their possibilities are shown partly by what we have already said about the children's social play. Their solitary and social play are beginning to be hard to separate, although we would expect solitary play to be more complex because the child does not also have to get on with other children. Getting on with someone else usually involves acting at a lower level. That is the nature of social life.

The very great step forward in this year is the invention of the *imaginary character*. Remember at age one children imitate adult activities; at age two they become an adult (parent); at age three they put some personality into it (an angry parent); but now at age four they become an imaginary person (a monster). These new imaginary creatures and imaginary companions let children extend themselves into all sorts of activities that are not a part of the usual run of events. They can consider both forbidden behavior and impossible behavior. Their imaginations are of great service in keeping their minds abreast of everything both possible and impossible. As long as they have this facility, they are not being closed off into one little channel of acceptable thought.

Throughout most of history cultures have conspired to take children and force them at this time into one traditional or conventional form of fantasy that would encompass all their own dreams—namely, the myth and ritual life of that culture, which its people felt was necessary to their survival. But in modern society we have a much larger problem for the imagination, and we must begin to look at that in the next chapter.

9 | The Dream:

From Five to Seven Years

A ghost and a monster came and got me and took my clothes and pajamas and got my father and took his clothes and pajamas and put us in a machine. I was so scared I woke up.

•

"Do you believe in matrimony?"
"Yes, as long as it has cheese on it."

When they are five, if not before, children go to school. At school the teachers show them how to get on with their school work. In the playground the other children teach them how to compete. On television the cartoon figures tell them that the small people eventually win. The years between five and seven are, therefore, an initiation rite into working and winning. By seven most children are beginning to know what this group myth is all about.

During their first five years children develop a private imagination, which we will call their dream. This dream consists of their unique feelings about themselves and their family life, and it will stay with them forever. But if we are not careful during the years of five through seven, this dream will no longer persist as an active force in their life. It will be pushed under by the group dream of winning and working.

As parents we have to try not to let our children lose this individual imagining. We have to find ways for them to tell their own stories, paint their own pictures, construct their own worlds, act out their own scenarios, and keep their own dreams alive. If we encourage their imagining, the new ways of working will become attached to their private way of feeling, creating a sense of self-discipline. Without that development they cannot take their dream forward in a productive way but must simply adopt the stereotyped dreams of the larger society.

This book is an argument against the older form of initiation solely into the three R's and good behavior. That initiation neglected the creative contributions that individuals have to make to the society in which they now live.

146

GAMES AND OTHER THINGS TO DO

The Morning Dream

The first source of all our creativity is the dream. We can ignore them or pay attention to them. Your children like to tell you about their dreams at breakfast. The dreams they tell you about are usually scary, which is why they want to tell you about them. We know from scientific studies that if you wake children up during the night, most of their dreams are not scary. This means that they only tell you these scary dreams because they want to get some help.

Many of the dreams of five-year-olds are like monster movies. The monster chases, captures, bites, and hurts them, and they try to escape but wake up feeling scared. They want to know that you love them and that they do not really have to worry about these night terrors. As children get older, they remember these dreams less, but they never finally leave them. Even adults remember these dreams now and again. As we get older, we do not forget these crises in our dreams; we just add new crises. If our lives are reasonably comfortable, however, we also add new assurances within the dreams themselves.

What are you to do? First, we think you should listen sympathetically. Tell children that dreams are stories about their feelings and that we all have such feelings. Dream-telling sessions around the table are reassuring to five-year-olds. It means that they are not alone in their dreams. Others are interested. It is only honest to realize that you yourself as the powerful person in the home are a part of the substance of their dreams. These are dreams of power. The children are dreaming of dangerous powers they cannot manage. For you to welcome and listen is to show that at least you personally are not as dangerous as the dream might suggest. But, as we have said at other times, listen quietly. Do not give lectures or in other ways show more of the same power that the dreamer is worried about.

Listening is only a first step. Listening is being receptive. It is making a safe place, a harbor to which the child can come after the rough night's voyage. After a time, days or weeks, of careful listening, if you feel the child is showing more confidence than fear about these dreams, then you can take a more active approach. There is a tribe of Malaysian people who actively explore their dreams every day. Everybody tells their dreams of the day, and everyone else gives advice on how to deal with them. If the dreamers are wronged in their dreams by anyone in the village, then those villagers give a present to the dreamers to show that the enemy they dreamed of must indeed have been someone else.

We are not suggesting that you begin to serve presents for breakfast. But this practice does suggest that the dreamers may need reassurance from the ones who are pictured as offending them in the dream. If those persons are at the breakfast table, why not give that reassurance. "Wow, I was a monster in your dream. That's me. I'm a monster sometimes. But I also love you," with a hug. We all have conflicts about those with whom we are closest. It is better to admit that there are two sides of the conflict, the love and the hate, than to pretend that only one always prevails.

This Malaysian group does another interesting thing. They tell the dreamers that the next time they meet the monsters in the dream they should tackle them without fear. They should go to them (in their dream) and make them give the dreamers a gift of a poem or a story that they can bring back to their tribe. Obviously we cannot lay that burden on five-year-olds without a lot more practice and village support. Still there is a principle here. After hearing their dreams, we can begin to discuss them. What were the monsters like? What color were they? How big? How did they move? Let us discuss monsters thoroughly in a vivid way. What are all the images we have of them?

Here we are, in effect, bringing out the images that lie behind creativity. We are focusing on, and extending, the children's attention to the creative aspects of their own dreaming. We are supporting the Malaysian idea of using the dream creatively. There is no reason why we should not tell our children this story of the people who go back into their dreams the next night and chase their monsters. The confidence of this attitude, the healthy view it suggests of one's feelings about oneself, is certainly no worse than the strange uneasy silence that usually accompanies most dream telling. The outdated view that the dream is a form of mental illness is not much use to children.

So let us become involved with these dreams, listen to them, discuss them, and then go on to have fun with them, because the next step after we have laid down this background is to begin to play with them. "OK, so the monster went after you. How could you have gotten away?" or "How could you have captured the monster? Then what would you have done?" Very soon your child makes exaggerated suggestions that turn the tables on escape and anxiety. When we are doing this, we are playing with the morning dream and are back into the mode of this book. Taking the anxiety out of dreams and putting play into them is to our minds a way to enhance their very real contribution to our creative lives.

Telling Stories

We hope that you and your children will gain something from dream telling. You can do the same thing with stories more directly. Here we go right into absurdity. Remember this is the age when cartoons begin to take over, and children are exposed to, and revel in, all the magical devices that are so frequently used in them. Bodies are expanded, shrunken, or changed into animals. People can fly in the air. As long as we are reasonably sure that the small heroes will always win, we will tolerate anything. Because the cartoon guarantees that the hero will conquer all, then the transformations become entertainable. "Guarantee us what is certain, and you can do anything you wish" seems to be the principle of this age.

The stories your children will tell now are usually very aggressive or violent from an adult's point of view. But if we think of what they have to deal with in their dreams, we realize that their stories only respond to their fears. In stories children see themselves mainly as attacked and afflicted by others. They are more often bailed out by parents and other amiable figures than they are in dreams. It is interesting to ask children, "How else could it happen?" and all kinds of creative suggestions can follow.

> IF . . .
> there were no monsters in the world
> there were no people
> people walked on their hands
> dogs made noises like pigs
> stars could land in your backyard
> mothers had five arms
> they held school on a boat
> you were your father
> you were a girl (boy)
> you never had to say thank you

Begin gradually with light, entertaining suggestions for different ways of looking at a story your child has told you. Then begin to make the suggestions more serious and then more radical, always taking your cues from what your child has suggested. We already talked about what you can do with wacky fairy tales. See what could happen to Snow White if she had to marry one of the dwarfs. Which one? Why? Suppose Rumplestilskin got his foot stuck in the floor and had to stay there forever, being fed by the miller's daughter. What if Rapunzel had used a protein cream rinse on her hair and the prince could not make his way up through the silky smooth hair? The same kinds of variations you made with nursery rhymes and fairy tales can lead to even more-creative personal storytelling.

Improvisation

In many ways this whole book has been about improvising. We have asked you as parents to make funny faces and funny noises to your babies. We have you walking around the floor on your hands like a horse. We have you croaking as the frog prince in the back of your throat: "Ribit, ribit, ribit." You have been asked to be an actor on the home stage. We feel that there is an important connection between your acting and your children's becoming versatile. All the time you are giving examples of being a very flexible person, and the children are learning that from you.

When they have reached five years of age, there are a series of steps you can make in improvisational games with your children. These steps follow the same steps taken by children in their own make-believe play from the age of one year onward. The first step was simply to create *make-believe* movements. You can begin to do this as early as three years. This is when you and your children or you and a group of children all pretend to walk around heavily like elephants or lightly like pussy cats; or you pretend to jump over the river, walk tall like skyscrapers, or walk small like bugs. This is a movement and music game that you can do with a drum.

The children's next step, when they were two, was to play

with a doll or toy and give it personality. Our parallel step at five is to pretend to play with an object. But we do not have any real object, so we use an *imaginary object*. We pretend to carry a heavy weight across the room; we are carrying the grocery bags from the car to the kitchen; we pretend to hammer a nail into wood; we pretend to cut with scissors.

As a first step children usually make a part of their body into the object they wish to imitate. Thus, when they cut with scissors, they make their fingers into the scissor blades. By about seven or so they will increasingly act just as if they were really holding the handle of a pair of scissors and make us imagine the blades. It is the same with the hammer. Younger children make their hands *be* the hammer. Older children make their hands *hold* the hammer. After a little warm-up a natural game is to take turns at reacting to, or using, some objects, while the others have to guess what you are doing. A large group of rather shy children can do it together in pairs; one watches while the other acts the part. This way you get the more customary informal play setting, and children do not feel so shy about being watched by an audience.

By the time children are three, they pretend to be somebody, usually a mother, a father, or a policeman—somebody who is important to them. Children's first pretense has to do with those actions that they identify with the person. Thus, a parent at first may be one who makes beds, shops, washes dishes, cleans floors, and has parties or one who rides off in the car or takes a load of dirt in his truck. Fathers are usually harder to define by actions because little children tend to see their actions less. There is the classic story of the little boy who acted his father by driving off on his tricycle to the city, coming right back, lying down on the floor, and saying, "Now I'll take a nap." (When children are five, they begin their improvisations of people first with similar obvious role-defining actions. The traffic cop signals on the traffic. How does he do it? The fireman turns his hose on the fire. What does that look like? Here they are being an *imaginary character carrying out routine actions*. Again, we can take turns at guessing who they are by their actions.)

In addition to imitating people they know, three-year-old children will also create *situations* in their play. The mother works in an office. The father runs a gas station. So in improvisation we move on next to *imaginary situations*. We want to know now not only who the person is and what they are doing but also *where* they are.

In their own play by the age of four children add some emotion to their characters (the mother gets angry at her baby), and after four they begin to create imaginary characters, such as monsters and Snow Whites. Thus, in our improvisation in the five to seven age period we can also add these two requirements. Now show us *how the person feels*. Show us a happy person, a sad person, an angry person. Show us someone feeling something, and we will guess what it is. Now be an imaginary person, and we will try to guess what it is that person can do, because imaginary persons can do imaginary things. But with this last step we have come to the end of this age period.

Certainly between five and seven children can do imaginary actions, react to imaginary objects, be imaginary people doing routine things, provide an imaginary setting, show emotion, and in some cases be completely fantasy people. They do these in the typical home game and take turns guessing what it is they are doing. Where there is time, this sort of improvisation can be extended so that children work together to present "plays" that they have made up. We think it is important to go slowly here. Between five and seven children are easily embarrassed by the idea that they are acting for someone else to see, which is why puppets work so well. At the same time they do want to be able to act for an audience. What gives them, or for that matter any of us, a feeling of safety is that they know there are clear rules, which is why ring games work so well.

This does not mean they will not be able to put on plays. After weeks or months of fairly anonymous plays, many children will get the feeling that there is security in this form of expression. Eventually they will want to introduce the plays that they create on their own into the new forum that you have created. What we are essentially doing through these games is creating a stage in our living room or classroom where imaginary things can happen. This stage is like their own personal play spaces. It is familiar. It is safe. The people there are trusted and, consequently, the children feel free to be inventive.

Television Talk

A major force in our day for making children into adults is television. There is so much of it and it changes so often that we might despair of ever knowing what is happening. But, in fact, the types of characters that children watch on their own shows and in cartoons pretty much play out the same characters as we have been giving them in folklore throughout the ages.

As parents we have to know a little about this in order to take part in the TV game. We have to know that the major lesson being taught children between the ages of four and seven is to *be shrewd* but stay nice. Do not be misled by appearances. Things are not always what they seem. Do not be gullible. Clowns are stupid people, always tripping over themselves. The moron asks silly questions. The tricksters are the smart puppets, smart in one way but foolish in some other. There are the impulsive honey-eating animals whose gluttony leads them into a fix, like Pooh Bear stuck in the hole.

Children learn that powerful people can be foolish, that small people can be foolish, and that what that means is that there are rules for grown-up behavior. You should not be gluttonous. You should not be one-eyed, trying to take everything away from everyone else. You should be sociable. You should share. These are simple lessons. But judging by the enormous amount of time that children spend watching shows that have these meanings, the lessons seem to take a long time to learn and to believe in. Actually we are usually more out in the open about telling children to be nice (do not fidget, yell, stare, spit, etc.), but we seem to have to use clowns, animals, and cartoon monsters to teach them how to be shrewd.

The TV game is really a game of conversation, of being able to play some of these roles yourself. For example, pretend to be the boastful clown who can walk on any tightrope anywhere, and then trip over the carpet. Just as this piece of buffoonery illustrates that pride goeth before a fall, most of the clowning appreciated at this age also illustrates one proverb or another. You can use proverbs as a cue to what to do. What is great for your children in all this is that you actually are their parent, whom they know 365 days a year, but you can take time out to enact a drama. You are versatile. Play the game of a blowhard, a self-booster. Think of ways in which you can take turns at acting it out and coming to disaster.

Play the game of gullibility. Even as early as four children understand this in game form. You let them trick you over and over. Each time they reassure you that if you show them, say, a coin in your hand, they will not take it, but of course they always do. Then you rough and tumble to get it back. They innocently profess only to want to examine it carefully, but, swipe, they have taken it again. So it goes.

On Being a Play Manager

Whether you like it or not, by the time your children are five you often find yourself not just playing with them but being in charge of a group of neighborhood or schoolchildren. What do you have to know? First, children have quite different styles of play, and they should not always be expected to like the same things. There are those who are mainly concerned with construction (science, cars) and impersonal kinds of play, and others who like dramatic and social play (houses, stores, schools). There are some children who are not really happy unless they are struggling with the physical environment, and yet others who prefer sedentary card and board games. There are highly impulsive children who move quickly from one activity to the next, and there are highly reflective ones who can stay with one activity for hours on end. There are those who like routine imitative play and those who prefer very imaginative improvisations. There are "boys" and "girls," "houses" and "trucks," "mothers" and "cowboys," "gymnasts" and "horses."

At the age of five most of the children's information is still coming from the adult in the group. The parent, teacher, or older child is still the major source of influence. It is wrong to think that in a large public setting freedom is enough for all these varieties of play. It is enough only if it is peaceable. There is no place for the hands-off policy that makes some children constantly the victims of others who have different play patterns.

Adults should understand that there are different types of play patterns and know how to make constructive suggestions and when to participate. Where children are impulsive and active, it often helps to limit the array of play materials that are set out. Play along with them for a while with the material that is put out. This fosters their own play with such materials. Sometimes, for example, a group of children may completely ignore blocks for months on end. It is only when the adults get block play going, by showing what they can do with blocks and the make-believe things they can make, that some children learn how to get involved.

You should introduce new materials and equipment gradually. Before children are ready to play, they should learn to master the equipment you are putting out for them. We have mentioned mastery through exploration, testing, imitation, and construction. There are steps within each of these types of mastery that children always go through on their way to play. These stages are universal at any age and in any situation. The astronauts learn to cope with their new environment in exactly the same way.

An example of the stages through which one- to two-year-old babies proceed follows. When they first see something new, say a block, they either are frightened and turn away or watch it carefully for some time. When they stop being frightened, they examine it carefully. Then they try to do something with it. This is their first attempt at mastery, and what they do will be one of the *actions* below. They explore how it relates to other objects (they bang the block); they see what they can do with it (they throw it on the floor); they copy what their mother does with it (they put it on another block); they build with it (they stack it along with several others in a tower). If they like the effect of what they have done, they will usually *repeat* this action for a long time until they have mastered it.

There is an enormous amount of repetition and practice in young children's mastery activity, but the same is true of adults, especially when we are learning a new skill, such as typing, skiing, or tennis. It often takes the example of a new physical sport for us to realize what babies have to deal with. When that skill is mastered, it is usually *combined* with other skills into something more complicated. They may begin throwing the block at the tower and toppling it over.

The phases, then, that mastery goes through are examination, action, repetition, and combination; and this is what most preschool free activity is composed of. Knowing all this, the wise organizer puts out only a few things at once and allows a generous amount of time for the children to master new "toys" before expecting the equipment to be used for active play. This is true for all types of equipment, whether it is clothes for drama, puzzles, household toys, store toys, or school-type toys.

Another reason it is important not to put out too many toys at one time is that children will cooperate well if they do not have duplicates of each other's toys. If they do have the same toys, they will not have to work (play) together. Everyone is his own cook if there are cooking toys for all. But if they have to share bowls and egg beaters, then they exchange and develop complementary roles. One is cook, the other sets the table, etc. Another consideration is that a teacher may have to direct overflow children to another play place. Thus she needs attractive alternatives. Crowding can ruin group play, just as it ruins most other things.

We hope that it does not sound as if we are advocating the turning of play into teaching. The art of the play teacher is to provide examples, and such teachers succeed only when children are mastering and creating their own play and games in their own way. The play teachers' skills are to martial resources and children, to know when to suggest taking turns or sharing, and when to become involved themselves in the play (for example, when to take a part in a play or to suggest that someone else try that role).

THE CHILD'S OWN PLAY

For five- and six-year-olds it becomes even harder to separate their individual and social play. This is partly because children prefer social play, so that their individual play is not as obvious to us. It tends to be restricted to the home or backyard, to the children's bedrooms, or even to fantasy. It becomes their own private world. Individual play or fantasy is very important, even though it is less accessible. As a general rule children are more advanced in solitary play than in social play. Individual play ideas appear a year or so earlier in individual play than in the children's social play.

In the last chapter we traced the various ways in which children get together and stay together. During this age period they are better at it. The same principles apply, but they pull it off with more success and for longer time periods. This is a great age for playing house, babies, school, cowboys, war, cops, doctors, dentists, funerals, ghosts, and witches. Often more than two children will get together for a long time, although several neighborhood children or nursery school children who have become familiar with each other will get along better or there must be an older child with ideas and power.

The group members have to learn how to play in unison, using a common theme, copying another member or some central person, and agreeing about who gets in and who is excluded. They have to cooperate and decide routines for what to play next and who owns what. All these skills demand playing together rather than simply alongside each other. If one is father, another is mother. If one is cop, the other is robber.

When the children were younger, they wanted to be the boss rather then take their turn and fit in with the roles that society demanded. The one exception, of course, was parent and baby, which were two fitting roles they knew very well and could practice much earlier. Between five and seven we move into the fitting roles that society is made up of: the seller and the buyer; the teacher and the student; the doctor and the patient; the cop and the robber; the husband and the wife; the soldier and the enemy; the mourners and the dead.

In the last chapter the games of order and disorder that come at an earlier age were unison games. The balance between order and disorder was played out by all the players. They all danced around, and they all fell over in "Ring around the Rosy." That fitted the capacities of children up to five, which is mainly to be able to do things in an orderly way together. Children between the ages of five and seven learn to play two different roles within one game. Playing different roles is characteristic of both their informal play (house) and their formal play ("The Farmer in the Dell"). Some types of games are organized around fitting two roles together like this.

Games of Acceptance and Rejection

For centuries small children of five to seven years of age have played ring games in which one person in the center got to act in a special way. The best-known modern example is "The Farmer in the Dell," where the person in the center gets to choose the next person to come into the middle with her. So the farmer chooses a wife, and the wife chooses a child, and the child chooses a dog, etc. In most, but not all, of these games the choice had a romantic implication. In the traditional game "Pretty Little Girl of Mine" a circle of children marched around the player in the center with their hands linked. As they moved, they sang the following lyrics:

> Oh this pretty little girl of mine,
> She's cost me many a bottle of wine.
> A bottle of wine or anything too,
> To see what my little girl can do.

> Down on the carpet she shall kneel,
> While the grass grows in the field.
> Stand upright upon your feet,
> And choose the one you love so sweet.

The player in the center imitated the actions of the verse while the others walked around. At the end that player chose another person, who then took his place in the middle, and the game was repeated. Most children still get some fleeting experience with these kinds of games, although ring games are not played as often by children today. They are still played a great deal more than most adults suppose, however.

It is clear that marriage and love are imitated obliquely in these games. What is more important about them, however, is choosing and being chosen to go into the center. Here in game form is the experience of acceptance and rejection that we spoke of in the last chapter as inclusion and exclusion. This is perhaps the most important question of childhood life. Do I get in or do I get left out? Will I be chosen to go into the center or will I be forgotten?

We all recognize the question in adolescence, when dating comes along, and in adulthood, when marriage is involved. Think of the bad breath and body odor industries, which are based on our conflict over whether we will be accepted or rejected. It all begins with the inclusion and exclusion activities of three-year-olds. But between the years of five and seven it takes on more of a romantic coloring. Even when girls alone are playing the game, many of the words have to do with lovers, kings, dukes, and wives.

Traditionally girls have worried more about this particular conflict than have boys, because marriage was more traditionally the only road for them. Therefore, they played more of these games of marriage. But as we found in our own study, even today little girls of three who come from professional families are more concerned than are boys with being accepted and not being rejected. Between the ages of five and seven girls can give you better information than can boys on who is friends with whom in their school classes. Thus, things have not changed too much, even though there may be fewer ring games.

In older times (and not so old times) the same girls who played marriage games when seven years old would be fostering kissing games at their parties when thirteen years old, and those kissing games had exactly the same concern. Do I get accepted or rejected? Can I get the lover I want? In order to protect the players against the outcome the thirteen-year-old games always relied on chance, as in spin the bottle. It was not your fault or responsibility if you had to kiss the other player. It was the bottle that did it. But by age fifteen the same group might be playing flashlight, in which all the couples sit kissing in a circle in the dark and the leftover player has to shine the flashlight on them. If that player finds anyone not kissing, the person with the flashlight gets to take that place. Here you make a choice, but the game allows you to give it up if you make a mistake.

Although today children do not express their apprehension about acceptance and rejection so often in ring games, they do tend to show it more clearly in informal conversation about boy and girl friends. They also show it in informal games of chasing, in which the girls chase the boys or the boys chase the girls, at the end of which there is grabbing, capturing, and sometimes kissing. These games begin between five and seven years and may be played throughout childhood, getting more boisterous and rough until about twelve years. After that age children show more earnest concern for acceptance on grounds of personal appearance, adequacy, and the like.

Chasing and Escaping

After all the one-sided and imperfect games of chasing during earlier years, we finally arrive at tagging or hide and seek, in which children clearly understand that there are two fitting roles (hider and chaser) and that they must take them one at a time. What is interesting is that although there are two different roles, as in the marriage games, one role is the more important one. The central person in this game, like the central person in "The Farmer in the Dell," gets the game going. Most children's games are like this until about the age of nine years.

Children seem to borrow from adults the-strong-versus-the-weak power relationship. The farmer chooses, the player who is "It" chases, and the weaker character gets chosen or gets chased. Hence, children's first game societies are a bit like their own experiences of being children with adults, except that in the games the children do play an important role. If they get chosen or caught, then they become the central people; and in the games they can at least escape if they hide well enough.

If you play these games with children, you have to soften your role a little by being a bit of a bumbler or a clown. You have to be a monster, but not too dangerous or too effective a one.

Attack and Defense

Children between five and seven years do not play games that use the strategies of attack and defense; these games are not played until about nine years, when games such as dodge ball, in which you actually throw a ball at the other person and that person has to dodge, become very popular. But we get forerunners of such games in cops and robbers, cowboys and indians, and witches and ghosts. These games consist of a mixture of chasing and escaping, as well as pretended attack and defense.

What is interesting socially is that these games are the first example of two *groups* of children playing against each other. Although the groups are small, maybe only two on a side or one versus two, they are the beginning of *teams*. Here children are not only fitting roles together (chaser and escapee) but also fitting groups together (friends and enemies). Not surprisingly in these games, the major activity is usually taking prisoners. The territory of the game becomes divided up into the safe place where one can hide and the dangerous place where one can capture others or be captured oneself.

Sex Differences

Traditionally there have been important sex differences in all these types of games. Girls have usually been more concerned with exhibiting order, boys with disorder; girls with acceptance-rejection, boys with attack-defense; both with chase and escape. In western culture we are at a point of reassessment of all of these and other differences. The more "passive" roles usually ascribed to women are being questioned. These sex differences have been learned ones, and what can be learned can be unlearned. It is only thousands of years of tradition that make particularly subtle the ways in which we teach traditional sex differences.

Although there are many complex questions that we do not have answers for, there seems no doubt that we should stop encouraging passivity and a sense of inferiority in girls. We should also stop demanding an impassive toughness from young boys. Neither of these is of much use in our culture today. There is no reason, however, why in your games around the breakfast table you should not at times exaggerate the worst excesses of both roles—for example, taking turns at portraying the ineffective weeping heroine and the swaggering brute. Such ribaldry and horseplay promote the growth of individuals. The idea of group conformity kills it.

10

The Absurd:

From Seven to Nine Years

Mary had a baby and named him Tiny Tim.
Put him in a bathtub to teach him how to swim.
Timmy swallowed water. Mary called the doctor.
In came the doctor, in came the nurse,
In came the lady with the big fat purse.

•

"What did one flea say to the other as they went off for a stroll?"
"Shall we walk or take a dog?"

•

Kirk takes his first train trip. He goes to the toilet. The conductor calling out the stations cries, "Dunkirk." The boy cries back, "Not yet."

By seven years of age children have acquired the main habits of the adults around them, and they have acquired the beginnings of important skills that they will need to survive in the parent society. Seven years is the time when children of many tribal societies become, in effect, small adults. They work in the fields. They look after babies. They do the cooking.

It is a time of responsibility. In the Middle Ages children were apprenticed at this age. In a similar manner we choose this age to teach children reading, writing, and arithmetic. At the same time we teach them the good habits of work, orderliness, cooperation, and competition. We expect them to be able to conduct themselves properly in school all day and follow all its multiple rules as well as to behave themselves on the playground, which is equally bound by rules.

The thing that saves their imagination during this high peak of social achievement is their rich sense of nonsense in the world about them. They perhaps need a clear sense of absurdity at this age so that by the time they are adolescents they can carry out original ideas.

GAMES AND OTHER THINGS TO DO

You will see throughout this chapter the way in which children of this age swing from rigid order to wild disorder.

Participation

As children reach the end of early childhood, which runs from birth until about seven or eight years, you can be flexible about playing with them. By and large children now have their own society, and they need you much less. You can participate more in spirit than in body. It is more a matter of making suggestions, of initiating ideas that are interesting and that might go somewhere. Your playfulness may now be just as momentary and interludial as was your three-year-old's with you some years earlier.

You can do this during meals, in the car on the way to school, or at any other time they can stand you. You can be a ham for the next two years and get away with it. But after that you will have to be more subtle. When accused of some injustice or infringement, you can sometimes pantomime your way out of accusations. "You said you would bring home a ball." "Well I got this big iron ball, and I carried it, and I carried it [miming], but it wore me out and I dropped it on my foot [hopping]. And if you go out in the car, you will find it on the back seat." You can still play dead, gasping and wheezing, as you receive a mafia bullet in the stomach. It is always the stomach because that is noisier. Breakfast or dinner allow hammed-up recollections of your own childhood. They are still acceptable, but not for much longer.

Sometimes hamming will help you through your refereeing and coaching role also. These are the years when children readily call one another a cheat, and just as readily cheat themselves, without being fully aware of the difference between their freedom and someone else's cheating. Larceny and righteousness reach an all-time high. You can make up a story of a guy who played just to cheat, with exaggerated examples of how he would have bare feet so he could pick up the other guy's marbles between his toes, how he would kick the marbles by accident, and how he would stick them up his nose to hide them, but one stuck and he rolled around in agony until the doctor came.

In games with your children you will find they are now sharper about winning and losing. They can be overwhelmed if you always win, but they do not want to see you always lose either. They know the difference. You can handicap yourself or you can play loosely and make mistakes. But there is a reality to contests of skill now, and it does children no good for you to fudge the difference. Their concern with skill is very real, and whether you are dealing with baseballs, jacks, jump ropes, marbles, cards, checkers, or dominoes, you should play with them fairly straight with mild but realistic effort. They have to know how to play. You can show them. They have to know what is fair and what is not. You can tell them. They have to see what skill looks like. You should show them.

Play, Playfulness, and Frenzy

We have said that there are differences between play and mastery. We should also distinguish between ordinary enjoyable play and that wildly inventive sort that occurs now and again. We could call this playfulness. In playfulness the players are more explosive than usual; they laugh a lot. There is a feeling of great fun as the player spins from one play idea or action to the next with great diversity and a freewheeling spirit.

Playfulness sometimes leads off into uncontrollable excitement, and a child gets to laughing and laughing and screaming in a way that is clearly out of control. This is not unusual during the first seven years. The feelings of self only gradually become stabilized and often are not enough to hold back the effects of overexcitement. A birthday party is a good example, and one that lasts throughout childhood. The additional stimulation and excitement of opening parcels leads in a crescendo through more parcels and to even higher expectations and fantasies. Thus, when children reach the end of the presents, rather than feeling pleasure they feel let down. Then there are tears and sobbing. Actually in the present situation what we have is not so much playfulness at the beginning as the mastery of novel things. Each novel object leads to higher expectation for the next novel object, and so on until there is no more.

But truly playful activities, like rough and tumbling, can similarly lead to expectations for greater stimulation, and children may increasingly throw themselves into the horseplay. Their usual control may break down so that they become almost frenzied with excitement. Their own feelings know no boundaries, and they are overcome with screaming, shrieking, etc. These extremes happen once in a while when children are being playful, just as they may get blue and depressed if they are *never* playful.

This is obviously a very complex subject, and we raise it here just to point out that there is an opposite maxim to our "If it isn't fun, forget it"; namely, "When fun becomes frenzy, forget it." Practically speaking, that may mean holding and calming your children, rhythmical rocking and singing to them, distracting them to some more-sober activity, distracting to some eating activity, etc.

Improvisation

Children are generally ready for stage behavior by now. Fantasy roles (Santa Claus, grandfather) are no problem. Portraying emotion is also OK. But more interesting is the stereotyped *exaggeration of character*. This is the time for children to overact. They can now begin to play the clowns that they have seen played by the Captain Kangaroos of the world. In order to play a clown, one must also have some sort of *plot*. The actor has to introduce the scene, develop it, and let it collapse. For children this may be little more than coming on stage, pretending to act seriously (for example, like a teacher), and then being unable to answer a question that gives away their abysmal ignorance. "Now let me see, one and one. That is very difficult. Perhaps I should look at the dictionary." The humor for this age is reaction to the sacred documents of the time: school books, dictionaries, time tables, poetry, etc.

Increasingly several children can take the stage and play out small dramas of their own. You can keep them informal, for example, by suddenly joining the group yourself as a visiting spaceman or as another character that will add interest and novelty to the plot. In a school classroom you can send in other children to join the action in roles that at first you suggest but later they add. "Can I be the grandmother?" "Can I be the owner of the house who makes them get out?"

What you are ultimately aiming for, but which will be difficult to achieve until about eleven years, is the kind of situation in which children can improvise before an audience. One child begins as one character, she is engaged by another character, but after some time both children begin to switch roles. Every time this happens the opposite player must adapt to the change. Children find it difficult to be versatile like this even at age eleven unless they have been well prepared during these earlier years.

In children's own play the same improvisation often takes the form of putting on stunts, circuses, and TV shows and making newspapers. They need you to provide material early in the game and to provide an audience later. When this sort of make-believe event is contrived, arranged, and presented by seven- to eight-year-old children, they are showing a capacity for cooperation and innovation that is way ahead of anything they have done the previous years and even more sophistication than has existed in their formal games.

Children are undoubtedly further ahead in this kind of play with friends than in their other forms of group play. Unfortunately, because we do not encourage this kind of play, children generally get worse at it as they get older in school, which means that they will have one less skill to think and feel with when they are older. To be able to improvise well is to have other ways of working through alternative actions and ideas.

Riddling

Children begin trying out riddles about the age of four; however, at this age these are simply silly questions without an answer that anyone can puzzle out. But that is the first step with riddles, asking questions that have an arbitrary answer. "Why did the man build his chimney?" "To see the bricks," says the four-year-old. By six years we are on to the favorite riddles of childhood, which are the moron-type riddles. "Why did the dog get out of the sun?" "He didn't want to be a hot dog." Riddles continue to be *the* favorite jokes of children for the next few years. After that age other kinds of jokes take their place.

Where do you fit in? Your role here is mainly to be patient. As far as we know, children enjoy riddles because they are a way of interrogating other people and of being superior at the same time; that is, unless someone else knows the answer. Throughout history many people have held riddling contests for adults. The societies that did so were usually ones in which older people spent time interrogating their young. Thus, the riddle, like much other play, is a way of reversing the circumstances. The child gets to be the one who asks the unintelligible questions.

When we remember that much of what we say to children must seem unintelligible to them, this exercise becomes more sensible. It is interesting too that riddles play with words in arbitrary ways. Riddles seem to say to us that what children find interesting is making nonsense out of words. Our words are often nonsense to them, but language has system. This game has system also. In the hot dog riddle the word "hot" means both hot by the sun and hot by cooking, and the word "dog" means an animal and a sausage. But the puzzle exists because the questioner acts as if only one meaning of "hot" and "dog" are intended.

The game to play at seven or eight years is to think of words that have double meanings and then use them as the basis for a riddle. In riddles we act as if words with the same structure (dog) have the same meaning (animal, frankfurter) when they do not. The lesson that children learn from this is again not to be gullible. So, for example, "What has ears that don't hear?" "Why, corn." In this riddle the corn's ears are not hearing ears. "What has feet that don't walk?" "A table." "What turns without moving?" "Milk." "What has a head that doesn't think?" "A pin."

A little later on children also begin to play not just with the double meanings of words but with the double meaning of things people do, as in the riddle about the fleas at the beginning of this chapter. Here the fleas have reversed the usual order of events. They are taking the dog. The dog is not taking them. Besides moron-type riddles with word or alphabetical meanings the other major type of riddle today is the riddle that is a parody. You expect to get a word puzzle, but you get something obvious. "What did the elephant say to the other elephant?" "Nothing. Elephants can't talk."

In sum, you can explain some of these principles. You can help them to make up riddles, and you can do your best to enjoy being the victim. It is not a bad idea to develop a family *groan*. This is the "Ohoh" with which all members greet a corny joke. The groan acknowledges the joke, but lets the listeners keep some distance from its awfulness. We are all familiar with its use with pun makers at a later age. Punsters inflict double meanings upon us, whereas riddlers merely search them out.

The groan is useful too for that new form of exactness that children start to use now. You are playing cards with them, and you say, "Why did you smash up the cards?" "I didn't smash them up." "You did so." "I did not. I only bent them." The other side of knowing double meanings through riddles is to become aware of what words actually say, so that those who speak loosely can be untied.

Nonsense

Just as riddles are based on children's now having some understanding of the meaning of words and letters, so nonsense requires that they understand the rules of behavior. From four to seven we have been putting them together as social and acceptable human beings. There has been a lot of group pressure there. Children of seven and eight gain some play freedom from all that by reversing the meaning of everyday events.

> Thirty days has September,
> April, June, and November.
> All the rest eat peanut butter,
> Except grandma.
> She drives a Buick.

Children begin to enjoy nonsense about authority figures because the orderly world that they have now accepted is run by authority figures. At the end of the school year it is "no more spelling, no more books, no more teacher's dirty looks"; it may be the character "Shut-up" who gets to the police station when "Trouble," his friend, is lost. "What's your name?" "Shut-up." "Are you looking for trouble?" "Yes."

More recently the cruel jokes have paraded before us a whole group of hardhearted mothers who seem not to care about their children's dire predicaments. These jokes have gradually slipped from adulthood to the upper reaches of this age group, nine and ten years. "Mother, I don't like this tomato juice." "Shut up kid, and drink your blood."

As a parent you probably cannot deal with this kind of thing unless you accept that this is not a perfect world. Even the good things create frustrations. Even the things we want to keep and sustain can also be a bore and a nuisance at times. The happiest way to deal with our very natural conflicts is through humor and play, and at this age children are excited by these and other forms of humor that make the sensible seem momentarily nonsensical.

Your role is usually a mixture of the participating ham and the referee. You share some types of nonsense, and you argue that other types are going too far. How far too far is depends on your own value system. But the technique here is the same technique as for all play; namely, that there can be a special time and place for being funny. That may be the only place for certain forms of humor. What you can say around the table you may not be able to say in school or to your neighbors.

If you do not feel comfortable in dividing the world up in this way, then this book is not for you. It preaches versatility, and sometimes the only way to be many people is to be them in separate places. The tie that binds people to themselves and to each other in this book is the general respect for, and enjoyment of, a life that can be shared, that is interesting, and that does not hurt anyone in any fundamental sense. The other tie that binds is the realization that love does not endure easily without laughter.

Pastimes

Children now have increasing numbers of pastimes that you can share in one way or another. They are into collections—stamps, postcards, license plates, hockey cards, jokes, lists of friends. These are interesting ways in which they manage parts of the world. Children who have stamps, for example, have a system for controlling the world. Their stamp collection is a construction that deals with the world in a particular way. It is not unlike a corporation in that sense. It is also an exercise in putting things into groups or classes.

The interest in collections comes at age eight, when children have just acquired the ability to sort things out systematically in several ways. By then they can put all the red triangles in one group and the red squares in another without confusing them because they are both red. You can tell them about your own "loony" collections: insect legs for science, bandits' ears for the police, types of ice cream for your refrigerated house. This leads them to invent their own loony collections.

One way children play with gullibility now is by using *magic tricks*. If you teach a few of these (such as card tricks, mirror drawing, tic-tac-toe, hangman, and the like), it will be a great asset to them in their social life. Tricks lure the watcher into something. On their own level they like surprises, such as jumping out on people, telling jokes, pretending to be a monster. They wish they had the "magic" to order their own food in the restaurant, to give hot dogs to their friends, to have their room cleaned, to have a plastic man take their place at school. This enjoyment of both surprises and magic makes them hungry for "tricks."

At this age *children's drawings* are somewhat stereotyped, like their riddles and their games. They draw by the rules. You can introduce fun and flexibility by posing problems for them. How about a face that frightens? How is it different from a face that does not? How about a body that jumps sideways? How is it different from a body that stands still? Make mad people that are half people and half automobiles. In this way children have to put together their set ideas for people with their set ideas for cars, and that challenges them to try something new. Doing cartoon sequences is another good challenge, especially if it is something like walking up stairs, because they have to make their fixed body drawings different in the different positions on the stairs. This is hard, and it is something they do not usually do.

You can play *card* and *board* games for a really long time with your children at this age, if you can stand it. Most card games for seven-to-nine-year-olds involve simple comparisons between cards. In war the two players take half the cards each. They turn up one card each at the same time, and the player with the highest card number takes both. Players aim to win all the cards. In grab players similarly put down their cards together, and the player who calls "grab" first when two cards are of the same value takes all the accumulated cards.

The board games of this age are Ludo, Chutes and Ladders, Parcheesi, and others, in which the players race each other toward a destination and the outcome is determined by the luck of the dice. Each rolling determines the number of steps forward they can take, but the board itself provides many hazards that either speed them forward or send them back to base. There is some minor decision making on the part of the players as to which counters to move forward or the like. Naturally they enjoy it also if you continue to join in all their other home play activities, including puzzles, Lego, blocks, collections, wrestling, tickling, music, cars, fixing things, word games, and chess.

Guessing

Finally we come to that key ability of this age, which most parents do not know about and do not realize is a critical part of children's developing intelligence—guessing. Here are some guessing games that your children may play and in which you can participate. More important, just seeing how many things guessing does for them opens it up as a tool for games that you would like to invent.

We mentioned that shrewdness was a virtue taught in the mass media during the previous age and throughout childhood. A key competence through which shrewdness must be expressed is *guessing*. In early childhood, from five to ten years, guessing is the everyday form of native intelligence. After all, one never has enough information at that age (or at any age), nor does anyone else that one relates to. So whether we call it guessing or not, we are always guessing. Guessing is putting together what little information we have with a little bit of luck in order to come up with the best answer.

Given the interest in guessing, there are dozens of games that you can invent. The simplest variety of games are those in which the player has to guess an initial, word, name, or color that the other player has thought of. Most popular is the universal I spy, in which players have to guess what the player who is "It" is thinking of in the room after being told what its first letter (or color) is.

There are many other such games. You have to guess where objects are hidden, which takes a lot of careful attention. In blindman's bluff you have to guess who you have taken hold of, which is guessing someone's identity. In some games you have to guess who is hiding the ball behind their back. The children have to keep their eyes on movements and guilty looks.

There are also a group of games in which players have to

guess what the others are acting out. One group of players acts a role; when the others guess it, they chase the first group. The names for these games are innumerable, although trades seems the most common. In trades the players divide themselves into two groups by choosing up. Then they line themselves up facing each other, about twenty to thirty feet apart. One group calls out to the others, "Here we come!" The second group calls, "Where from?" The others reply, "New York." Then the players of the second group ask, "What's your trade?" The answer is "Lemonade!" The second group then says, "Go to work!" They begin to act out some kind of work, such as shoveling snow, picking cherries, planting potatoes, or whatever, and the second group tries to guess what they are doing. As soon as they guess it, the actors run back to their station, and the others chase them. If any of the actors are caught, they join the opposite side. The game usually continues until all the players of one group have been caught.

There are a number of children's games in which the player must guess in turn how many objects the other players are holding in their hands. Games like this have been named Hul Gul, How Many Eggs in the Bush? or Jack in the Bush. In one version each player is given an equal number of buttons, beans, grains of corn, and the like, and then each in turn holds out a handful to the guesser, calling "Hul Gul!" The guesser replies, "Handful," and then the first player asks, "How many?" If the number named by the guesser is too high, the guesser must give the other player enough counters to make the difference. If the guess is too low, the first player must give the guesser enough to make the guess right. If the guess is exactly right, the guesser gets the whole handful.

There are other variations of the game using fingers, odd or even amounts, and so forth. Although the game is ostensibly a game of guessing or chance, there is a minor element of strategy possible insofar as one can gauge the number in the other players' hands by how big their hands are or how big they make their hands. What is interesting about this game is that it requires close attention to numbers, especially to real differences between small numbers of objects. It was probably a good way of getting to know numbers before children regularly went to school.

Some Other Games

There are many many games we have not mentioned. But hopefully there have been enough to give you some sense of what to do and what it is that your children care about at this age. Let us finish by just mentioning a few other games you might want to play with them. In the car you can play games with points for all the different kinds of animals that you all see or for different kinds of cars or house colors. The first one to see the animal (or whatever) gets the points.

This is also an age for making finger shadows on the wall. It is one of their bag of tricks for creating illusions, not merely being taken in by them. It is probably the end of Easter egg hunts, although you can do new things with a kitchen orchestra of pans, combs, and buckets. Paper games (such as fortunes and paper planes) and practical jokes (such as "I saw a dead horse. I one it. You two it. . . . You ate it," sending someone for a left-handed hammer, or putting a toy snake or spider on a friend's desk) are popular tricks.

Games in which no one must laugh until the balloon strikes the floor or where you must stroke the kneeling players saying, "Poor kitty, poor kitty," without laughing or where you say, "The first to speak is a monkey," appeal at this time. Children are just beginning to use these games as ways of handling their own emotional control. To be provoked and yet keep from giggling is one more indication that one can obey the rules—not just the rules of the games, but the rules of how to keep your self-control. School has become much more of an institution and less of an adventure by now, which is part of the reason that paper games appeal. Rubber bands also create excitement at school, being flicked about or used to flick paper.

THE CHILD'S OWN PLAY

This is an age when children begin to acquire friends, and such relationships sometimes last for weeks and months and even years. This is more likely to happen if they live close to each other. When possible, children tend to choose others of the same age and sex and interests. But sometimes it does not matter all that much because they are not all that set in their ways yet.

What is often interesting in the play of seven-year-olds is how rigid their own rules are. We have seen that our adult society molds them into decent behavior. We have seen that in their nonsense and riddles they show some appreciation for the absurdity of these pressures. But in their own group play behavior they are often even more coercive than we are. They are much harder on each other. What they call being "fair" is often a one-eyed claim for their own point of view.

In a way, this is not surprising. We have seen how hard it is for children to get their groups together. Ever since we started our analysis of their social play at three, we have been documenting a rugged struggle. They have had to work out who was boss, and they have had to develop techniques for keeping together. In addition, they have had to work out many common themes and, with the beginning of games, common types of relationships (accept-reject) that are important in the larger culture and that they have to understand.

This is an age when rhymes and rituals seem to be a great help in their games. It is an age when they are prepared to pass harsh judgment on those who break the rules, even though they do not really observe them very well themselves. They do not realize this yet, however; although they lie without too much self-awareness, they condemn it as a major crime. In all of this they are helped by adults, who make rules very clear and who are very fair in enforcing them.

Often their game rituals stray over into *private rituals*, showing again a desire for *order* in their personal feelings just as much as in their social world with other children. Thus, "You have to be on your bed before the door slams or else *IT* will come out from under the bed and get you" or "You have to get upstairs before the toilet stops flushing or else *IT* will get you." Sometimes the child's precarious relationship with God enters into these private dramas. "If I get to the utility pole before the bus does, God will be kind to me."

Chasing and Escaping

At this age children are not satisfied merely to get away from the player who is "It" and then when caught to take that player's place. Now they like to tease that player too. Thus, in a game like kick the can, while the person who is "It" is chasing someone else, the other children run back and kick the can, letting everyone else go free; or in freeze tag they run around tagging the children that have already been "frozen," freeing them. It is an age for testing out what they can do against authority. Seven- and eight-year-olds begin to be "cheeky" in school. They say sassy things, and they know the language well enough now to make it sound silly.

There is a famous old game called ghosts in the garden that nicely captures the dualism of good and bad parents that children like to act out in their games at this time, although usually these days in ways that are more informal. It goes like this. The mother smacks her children and tells them to go and wash their hands. The children run out into the garden, see a ghost, and come running back crying, "Oh, Mommy, there's a ghost in the garden." The mother says, "It's only my pink pants on the line," and she tells them to go and wash their hands as before. They do so but come running back with the same complaint that there is a ghost in the garden. This time the mother says, "It's only Daddy's white pants on the line."

The same thing happens again, and this time the mother tells them to go and feel the pants. They run back crying, "Oh, it's got fur on it, Mommy." The mother says, "Come with me and I'll go and see." To the ghost she says, "What are you doing in my garden?" "Picking up sticks," he replies.

"What do you want the sticks for?"

"To light a fire."

"What do you want the fire for?"

"To boil a pot."

"What do you want the pot for?"

"To boil a stone."

"What do you want the stone for?"

"To sharpen a knife." (At this point the children scream.)

"What do you want the knife for?"

"To cut off your heads."

The ghost then chases the mother and the children, and the player who is caught becomes the next mother. In some versions the game finishes with a game of fox and geese, in which the mother tries to get her children back from the ghost (or witch or fox). The ghost stretches out its hands, the children hold on behind the ghost in a chain, and the mother tries to get around behind the ghost and tag the children. Those she tags are then free. In most versions the recaptured children get a good licking and are of course naughty and sassy with the mother. There are many other games like this (for example, Mother, Mother, the Pot Boils Over; Who Goes Round My Stone Wall; and Old Mother Gray).

There are other chasing games that illustrate this new *duality* toward authority. In cross tag the other players help the pursued player by passing between her and the person who is "It." The person who is "It" must then chase the player that passes in front of her. In caught and free the players not caught try to free those who are. They have to stand still but can be freed by a tag from the untagged players. This game is also known as pebbles and stones and as candlesticks. In cat and mouse the person who is "It" chases the mouse in and out of a circle of players, who aid the mouse by holding their hands when the person who is "It" tries to pass but lowering them for the mouse to go through.

Notice in all these games how harassed the "It" figure has now become. Clearly the children are expressing an independence of power figures that they will not show in their own behavior until preadolescence, several years off. The game allows them to experiment with revolution in its own limited way. But note that the game relationships are still one-sided. Some roles are more powerful than others. It will not be for a year or two yet that children go into games with strict equality before the law, as in baseball, football, etc.

Dominance and Usurpation

Chasing and escaping and the challenging of good and bad parents are one of the themes of the day. Another is being bossy and then having your position taken away from you. Two illustrative games will be discussed below. Traditionally these games were more often played by girls, suggesting perhaps that they were expected to be more interested in these forms of arbitrary power and status.

In steps and strides the person who is "It" is out in front at one end of a space. He calls out instructions to the other players, who are at the other end of the space. He tells them what they can do as they try to get down to where he is. The first to reach him becomes the new person who is "It." There is a terminology of movements; for example, needles (put the heel of one foot in front of the toe of the other foot), pin (move forward half a foot length), lamp post (go down on hands, feet staying where they are and hands stretching out as far as possible, and then stand up on point where out-stretched fingers reach), umbrella (whirl around and forward until commanded to stop), etc. The person who is "It" tells the number of steps to be taken in each case. This game is known also as giant steps and as cauliflower and cabbages.

Mother may I is the same game, except that the players ask what they can do. "Mother may I take five jumps?" "No, you did not say please." "May I take five jumps please?" "You may. No, you cannot. You did not say thank you." Here the game has a similar movement pattern, but the "It"-controlled bossiness has increased tremendously. Cheating seems to be the rule. "You can cheat by edging up when the leader is not looking." "They're supposed to be fair, but they often favor their own friends."

Correctness or Mistakes

We mentioned earlier that this is an age when children begin to understand competition, just as they understand work at school. They are now interested in winning, although they are frightened of too great a challenge. The most impor-tant games that girls usually play from this age onward throughout Western civilization are jump rope, hopscotch, ball bouncing, and jacks. In all of these games the aim is to progress slowly through a series of actions and not to make mistakes. That is what most girls remember about these games. They did not want to make a mistake as they entered the rope or as they threw up the jacks. Notice that in these games you do not really lose in any drastic sense. Each time you may carry on from where you left off the last time, the winner being the one to get through the whole series first. Everyone makes progress even if one player is the most successful.

Perhaps there is a relationship between the careful step-by-step progress in these games, the emphasis on not making mistakes, and being a traditional woman; that is, one who is concerned with etiquette and formal behavior, one who is frightened of mistakes, one who is not so much concerned with winning as with not breaking down. Girls will tolerate a less than competent player as long as she is amiable and brings something to the game. She could be a good rope turner or just a pleasant audience. A girl who fusses about not winning or is constantly berating herself for not being in form "today" is more likely to find herself hanging on the fringes, not invited to play. The society of the game has traditionally been more important to girls than the outcome has been, rather like afternoon women bridge players who will socialize more than the mixed sex evening groups, where the quality of the play and the outcome of the game is more important.

Some examples of these games follow. In jump rope two girls turn a rope over while others take turns jumping and others chant the rhymes. Some of the rhymes refer only to the speed of the skipping, usually requiring the child to speed up as the rhyme progresses.

> One to make ready
> And two to prepare,
> Good luck to the rider
> And away goes the mare.
> Salt, mustard, vinegar, pepper.

When the child trips on the rope, she goes out and the next child comes in, or alternatively she skips out when she has had enough. The rhymes refer mainly to things that girls are interested in, the occupations and interests of women.

Hopscotch is played on a diagram marked out on the ground. There are various kinds of diagrams: circles, rectangles, and rectangles with arms. In all games the child throws (or kicks) a stone or piece of wood into the numbered compartments in the diagram. If the marker does not land in the right square, the child is out and it is the next child's turn.

Ball bouncing is a solo performance by a player who tries to see how far he can get without a mistake. In competition players take turns to see who can get the furthest. It may be done with or without a rhyme. One such rhyme follows:

> Two, four, six, eight,
> Mary's at the garden gate,
> Eating cherries off a plate.
> Two, four, six, eight.

Children go through complicated gymnastics as the game gets more difficult.

Jacks is a game played with five small objects; for example, stones. The movements are very complicated and difficult. The first to complete the sequence wins. The movements include those in which a player throws the stones in the air with her right hand and tries to catch them on the back of that hand.

In all the games in this chapter the child is one player in the middle of a group of players. Generally we do not have one child competing directly with another at this age. That is too direct a form of competition. It is easier if one child plays among the others, so that although one may win, *all* the rest lose. This makes losing easier to bear. Marbles is like that. There are many other informal skill contests that children get into at this age: marbles, throwing stones at targets, spinning tops, or flying kites. There is an obliqueness to the issue. By nine or ten children are being asked to be more directly competitive, and for that reason we are then into another age.

We finish, as does the age, with its most famous poem, which begins as follows:

> Ladies and jelly spoons
> I come before you to stand behind you
> To tell you something I know nothing about. . . .

11 | Competence with Caring:

From Nine to Thirteen Years

At eleven she wants to be a herpetologist. We ask her why. "Because I like snakes better than boys." "You believe that a snake is a better companion than a boy?" "On no," she says. "After a snake comes a lizard, then a tortoise, then a gila monster, and then comes boys maybe." [Art Linkletter]

•

He enjoys the psalm:
  The Ford is my auto, I shall not want.
  It maketh me lie down in mud puddles,
  It destroyeth my soul. It leadeth me
  Into the path of ridicule for its name sake.

•

At twelve she has a party for eight girls and four boys. She orders forty-three hot dogs and five dozen bottles of Coke. Although the music is on, no one dances except a couple of girls. Then one girl runs round the block, and four boys follow her. They come back and drink one dozen bottles of Coke. Then the one girl runs round the block, and this time everyone follows her. They come back and drink two dozen bottles of Coke, breaking three bottles. [Margaret Mead]

•

She stretches out her arms stiffly and demands to know who put the concrete in her deodorant.

The important thing about children from eight or nine onward is that they want access to skill and technique. Prior to this they have been very happy with fantasy. They have taken their own dreams with them to school, and they were pleased to have the teacher wrap them up in legends and folktales. Up until the fourth grade teachers can often get their group to work hard on a task that is totally imaginary. For example, children can pretend that the classroom is a city, with one corner a shop and another corner the post office. They can build a make-believe monetary system, and some children can be make-believe accountants and some can be mailmen. Everyone can write letters to everyone and deliver them through the make-believe post office. The arithmetical genius can be the banker and issue credit.

Classroom make-believe of this sort can carry most of the curriculum if the teacher has the heart for it. The wise teacher, however, usually knows that each such world-fantasy cannot be expected to last more than a month or so. Schools follow "seasons" just as games do. Next the teacher can convert the whole room into a publishing enterprise, and a month later into the mint, and after that into a ship at sea. The romance of early childhood becomes the romance of the world in the second to fourth grades.

But romance is followed by industry, application, and sobriety in most places where it is found, and childhood is no exception. What today we love, tomorrow we seek to control. This age then is a period of technique. Children are generally less spontaneously creative during this age period than they were earlier. They are often more interested in how to do things. They are interested in learning how to use tools and musical instruments and how to do crafts, leather work, bookbinding, weaving, carving, sewing, and metal work.

During this period they are able to sit still for concentrated periods of work, and they have the dexterity to accomplish these tasks. Fingers that can manage marbles or jacks can certainly be trusted with chisels and needles. The eleven- and twelve-year-olds often hunger for a real job and money-earning possibilities. They prefer visits to real wharves, factories, and newspaper plants; they want you to take them camping, riding, or on a cycling tour. In all of these activities children need help and guidance always, but they want their play to be "real" rather than pretend.

While their very real need for new skills should be satisfied, it must not be exploited. If we reduce skills to routines and allow no scope for children's imagination and playfulness, when adolescence arrives and creativity again yearns for expression, there will have been no continuity.

Much of our emphasis here will be on means of continuing creativity while at the same time satisfying skills. The unity of the two is the most important form of self-discipline children can get. The best evidence of this is the finding of one researcher that although most normal adults have much self-control, they have lost access to their feeling life. Conversely, disturbed persons have access to their feelings but have lost control. Artists, unlike either normal or abnormal people, both control and have access to their feelings.

This lends support to the view that a better way to think of bringing up children with self-discipline is after the manner of a person who is schooled in the arts, rather than the earlier, accepted methods. In the arts we first allow much free expression with media in a preliminary way. Then, when children are thoroughly attached to the medium, we increasingly introduce technical skill. There follow the long rigors of personal application that are denied to most children because we have not known how to handle the preliminary period of romance for them. A home or school that followed the career of an artist as its model of growth might do much better than we have so far managed.

The model of growth that we sometimes follow is that of the Australian aboriginal initiation rite, where the old punish the young to keep them in their rightful place. Most often it is a watered-down version of the army or the church; in these disciplines it is the good of the organizations and the purposes they serve that are at stake. In the arts it is the expressive uniqueness of the individual that is at stake, which is why this chapter has been called "Competence with Caring." Parents can contribute to children's skills and help keep their trust in the authenticity of their own feelings by trying to enjoin their playfulness with the arts.

GAMES AND OTHER THINGS TO DO

Dreams

In their night dreams children become somewhat more active as a character. They are less often the victim. They might not yet be the victor, but often they will get help from others. There are fewer threatening monsters and more children in their dreams. More adults represent authority figures rather than monsters. The children sometimes cooperate together. The dreamers are concerned with their skill and their adequacy and whether a job was well done or not. Interestingly, the dreams of disturbed children show much less mention of other children and of authority figures but still show more of the terror of the five-year-old.

If you have not yet told your children how the Malaysian group handles their dreams, now is the time. By and large, however, unless dream telling and playfulness about dreams have become a way of life in your family, children will not often spontaneously tell dreams during this age period. Their increasing need for privacy, for independence of adult thinking and adult concern, usually leads to a less willing communication of intimate things. If you have continued discussing dreams and being creative about them, however, then the dreams will continue to be an occasional center of playfulness.

Perhaps the most important thing to say here has to do with listening to the feeling in a dream rather than to its contents. If you are welcomed to share your children's dreams, listen for its feeling or even ask, afterward, what the dream felt like. Of course, having said all this, we have to recall our earlier statement—that sometimes a child brings a dream to you simply because he *feels* terror and needs relief. In that case, you must be reassuring rather than provocative. "Remember," you say, "it is only a dream. I am here. The house is still here. You feel that way in the dream. But the daytime goes on. Perhaps next time you will feel stronger in the dream. Run harder or fight harder." Let your message of reassurance be carried over as a view that even in a dream one can fight back.

The question "what did it feel like?" is a key question for all creative work with children or with ourselves. "What did it *feel* like?"

Most of our everyday world is geared rather to asking what did something *look* like or what did someone *say*, or what did you *learn*. We tend *not* to ask what it felt like. We tend not to say, "Yes, I know that's what he said, but what did it make you feel?" Yet constantly in our relationships with others we "know" one thing but "feel" another, and just as constantly in our education we neglect the latter. But the latter is the source of our most personal responses and, therefore, of our own creativity.

A dinner table game in which players take turns can be "What did they look like and what did they feel like?" They looked like *this*, but they felt like *that*, with appropriate mimicry; for examples, "He looked like a stuffed shirt, but he felt like a zilch." The same duality can be asked of a dream. "What happened and what did it feel like?" Usually, however, dreams are more of one piece, so the question may be unnecessary. The things that happen in the dream are pictures of the feelings we have anyway; they mirror our feelings. Perhaps that is why we need them. We do not get to picture our more basic feelings in other areas of our existence.

Improvisation

Up to this point in our improvisations with young children we have made believe that we were *moving* in some way, relating to an imaginary *object*, being an imaginary *character* doing routine things, and creating an imaginary *situation*. We have also played *fantasy* characters, characters with *feelings*, and *exaggerated* characters in some brief *plot*.

At this age the big step for children is to *interact* with others in dramatic activity. Up until this point children have interacted in their own group play, whether it was informal play or more-formal games. They have interacted also in group performances at home (circuses, carnivals) and have learned performances at school (history plays and the like). Past relationships with others have been diffuse and more like play than like characterizations.

If we have been working with improvisation, we have encouraged children to do things one-by-one, because this aids them in their concentration and allows them to develop a better focus on their own characterizations or imaginary actions. The presence of other children makes improvising very difficult for children up until about eight years. Other children infect them so strongly that they find it difficult to keep their characterizations in mind.

In one of our studies with Dr. Gilbert Lazier there was a scene in which a child finds a wallet with money in it and then a policeman comes on stage and demands that it be handed over. Up until about the age of eight years, the children could not handle this latter scene. It was too exciting for them. When the policeman demanded the wallet, they would cease to act and change quickly into a game of hide and seek, running away and screaming with the policeman after them.

Older children, whether they resisted or not, were able to handle the matter dramatically. They might resist, but they would do so with explanations and evasions rather than by breaking down into flight or laughter. Partly their new attitude is because from about seven onward children are much more able to use language to *organize* their actions. In addition, after the age of nine children are not quite as excited about authority figures as they were in earlier years; they have learned ways in which to cope with that problem, whereas five- and six-year-olds are just realizing that authority *is* a problem for them.

In any case, our new age, nine through twelve, is the age of social concern and social conformity, and this bodes well for improvisation that asks for roles to be played with and against other children. If one asks why it takes so long for interaction to be put on stage (age nine) after it has appeared spontaneously in games (age six) and group play (age four), we can only suggest that the stage is a much more complex and self-conscious place than are either a game or play. One has to consider the medium (the acting) and the audience, as well as one's immediate subjective feeling (as in play). We are not really talking about the theater stage in the formal sense. It is just that whenever you are explicitly asked to improvise something and others are watching you, you are in all essentials on stage. Any time children have to think both of what they do and of someone watching it, they are on stage in our way of putting it.

The easiest place to start is with the elements we have already mentioned: two characters showing by their movements what they are doing (one old, one a child), two characters relating to an object (both carrying a weight) or to a situation (a kitchen). These are the first and preliminary steps that can be acted out without words, and even younger children can handle this level of interactive complexity, just as they can handle speaking through puppets or telephones.

But what we hope to achieve from now on is something more complex. We want to see them act out characters who have feelings and who are in conflict with each other. We want to see them do fantasy characters interacting in an imaginary environment. Although in general we are just putting together the old elements in more-complex combinations, the addition of the element of conflict is most important. Working up to a *conflict* between characters and dealing with it after it has occurred is, after all, the essence of the dramatic plot.

At this point we come to a "conflict" in the views of those who advocate drama for children. There are those who think it should deal mainly with children's feelings; it should begin with the things they care about and let them act out those feelings. In this way the art form truly deals with problems the children have and is a living reality to them. "Plays" should be constructed around these feelings. This is often called psychodrama.

Then there are those who see drama mainly as an art form, and they say that what we have to do in improvisation is to teach children how to perform. They emphasize the discipline. They suggest, for example, that dealing with children's own conflicts leads only to superficial dramatic behavior. The children are mainly playing out their conflict ("one pretends to be the sheriff, the other the bad guy"), and they do not, as a result, really focus on the nature of the improvisation itself.

To help improvisation, it is further argued, it is better if each player focuses on some concern that they have with objective things. Thus, two players can both pretend to be unloading a station wagon. In this way their focus and ours as the audience is on the actions of arms and bodies and their relation to the wagon and the shopping baskets being carried. This focus keeps involvement in the nature of acting, not in other things. If conflict arises in the course of this careful improvisation (they start to argue about who pulls out a certain bag of groceries), then the conflict grows out of the actions rather than being only loosely expressed through them.

One finds this conflict between those who want to use the art form to motivate children for educational purposes and those who want to use the art form to train children to be artists in every art form. The first group is more concerned with immediate self-expression and with the participants' enjoyment. In music they like teaching to begin with the children's own free compositions. In graphics they prefer free activity with finger paints, clay, large brushes, and the like. In movement they like free interpretive activity to modern music. In writing they want personal accounts of the children's lives or their sense of adventure. In drama they prefer psychodrama to training in acting.

In recent years there has been a great deal of work with free expressive forms, both with preadolescents and with adolescents. Although the evidence is only anecdotal, it shows fairly conclusively that when these programs are well conducted, the children become highly involved in them and there is an improvement in their general behavior and their concentration on more-orthodox school subjects. In one group of adolescents who came from economically poor homes, over 90 percent of a voluntary youth drama group subsequently went on to college, whereas the usual college attendance for these children was under 10 percent.

The record also shows that the free expression stage is only a preliminary one. Depending on the group, the desire for such expression lasts a few weeks or a few months. The more disturbed or repressed the children, the longer the need for this initial period of using the materials in a highly personal and nontechnical way. In summer camps for disturbed children, for example, for months finger painting has to be body painting with paints and body smearing with clay before they are ready to attempt finger painting as an art form.

In drama at our preadolescent age level there is often a gross acting out of excretory functions and of violence in the earlier stages. This occurs because such feelings have never been on stage before. It happens because "rationality" has been restricted to reading and arithmetic and how to behave. Children have been taught how to control feelings but never how to express them with control. They have not been taught how to be rational with feelings. One young dramatics teacher we know uses the technique of having children go on stage and act out "their secret," which everyone else has to guess. The secrets chosen to be acted out by the group were "Don't bother me," "Failing a test in school," "Fuck," "Wanting to be a ballerina," "My name," "My shoes are on the wrong feet," "I have grown a moustache," and "I have a jar of candy hidden on stage."

If, however, children's feelings are freely allowed into their play activities, so that the children learn to handle them rationally, then explosive use of the art forms tends to be minimal. To handle feelings rationally means, in this context, to know how to express them in a socially valuable way. For example, when children have been allowed to mime their feelings as a regular part of their play life with adults, then when they are suddenly overwhelmed with annoyance, they may mimic their annoyance or mimic the person annoying them. In so doing they create laughter for themselves and for others, and their annoyance is not then turned into unmanageable anger. Alternatively, they may go off and write a limerick or something else. This is a rational expression of feeling.

We are not suggesting that people should not sometimes express anger directly. Rather, we are talking about a quite different problem; namely, that throughout history people have imagined that expression itself is irrational and that rational people inhibit their expression as much as possible. We so tend to believe this that in the past the normal response to children who handled their frustration by mimicking their host was to swat them over the head rather than to appreciate the "civilized" character of their response.

For most children in most places art begins as free expression but after a time moves into technical skill. It should be emphasized, however, that it is not just because children have been overcontrolled or because they are disturbed that art forms must begin with these resources in the children themselves. If this is not done, as children grow older they get more intelligent about art forms, but they do not develop any higher levels of aesthetic response.

In another study of our own we found that younger children of seven years, although not very communicative in the content of their paintings, used more color than did older children of eleven years, in their stories they used more-novel characters, and in their improvisation they were more involved in the acting. They seemed to a set of judges to put more feeling into their characterizations. The older children of eleven years or so were much clearer and more intelligible in what they did in all these media—painting, story writing, and drama—but they were relatively lifeless. As they grew older, they seemed to learn how to be more intelligible, but at the price of being less expressive.

This gain in intelligibility but not in sensitivity is not something that can be easily overcome. Ours is overwhelmingly an information culture. We double the total sum of knowledge every few years. Our political and scientific leaders require enormous amounts of information even to begin to make sensible decisions about the extremely complex matters that face them. It is very hard for even those who are in arts education not to find themselves spending much of their time making decisions about how to think about the arts rather than about artistic quality as such. Thus, it is not surprising that too early a grasping of the technical stage of an art form by children is likely to lead to expertness that has no depth in feeling, in which there is competence but not great caring. The whole thrust of our culture is toward the informed rather than the "sensible" mind.

Although nobody knows how long children should stay in the most personal and most expressive uses of an art form, it seems wise to argue that they should not be pushed out of them and into technicalities too early. Perhaps we can clarify our position this way. By the age of nine and ten years if improvisation has proceeded as advocated earlier, children will be able to handle some acting with others around conflicts and with some sense of plot. From here on there are a series of three stages, which you can have in mind, as the dramatization proceeds. The first two are quite personal; the third is the technical stage.

In the *realistic stage* improvisation is seen as a mirror of society. Up until about eight years of age children, when asked to "think" about art, pretty much see it in this way. The art is a picture of the way things are, whether they are talking about a painting or a dramatization. But there are two levels to this realism. The first level, which we have already dealt with, has them acting out the everyday lives of those about them ("This is the way we wash the clothes"). By the age of nine or ten we are ready for the second level, having them act out their own feelings.

This second level is where the psychodrama enters in, and so we have them act out such gross matters as an argument between siblings over which parents love each child most, a dispute between kids who come from rival neighborhoods, an argument between parent and child over whether the chores were properly done, and an argument between husband and wife about what to do with the kids (shades of "Hansel and Gretel"). Often, asking children to think of the time when they were most angry or sad touches off a theme for an enactment between two people. When the event is recalled, you as the parent, another child in the family, or another child in the class can play the other role.

In psychodrama there is a whole set of interesting techniques that involve such things as the players' acting out both their own role and then the role of the other person or the players' acting out how the other person is and other players' acting out how they are; or the players' acting out two sets of thoughts, first what they will do and second what they would like to do. The conflicts of feeling that children feel toward each other, toward parents, and toward teachers and that they get joy out of representing either realistically or in exaggerated form are endless. In some ways there is sufficient material here for the rest of your life.

In the *moralistic stage*, the second stage in developing our appreciation of art, lies the notion that the play or the picture has a message. Here we believe there is some meaning to it over and beyond what is simply to be seen there. Many children see art this way by ten years of age. Many adults never see art in any other way. Thus, this is the stage of soap opera. One of the tragedies of education has been that the sophisticated people who deal with the arts and abhor the lower forms have been reluctant to realize that there is an age in childhood when this is the most relevent form.

Making up improvisations that teach a lesson is a lot of fun and an excellent way of developing a sense of the rise and fall of plot and the conflict between characters. Inadvertently, many of the "historical" dramatizations that teachers have often used are of this nature. They tell a story. The simplest of these morality tales are fairy tales. If adequately dressed up, they are still acceptable. The "virtues" of Cinderella and the wickedness of the sisters can be exaggerated and played upon with great delight from nine onward.

At the prior stage of aesthetic development what we gained was the projection of personal feeling on stage. Children were able to represent themselves in action, even if in fairly gross form. What we get at this stage is the projection of self into character. By playing an exaggerated and wicked stepmother the child explores the nature of characterization. This is the time of life for being a ham on stage. Culturally we have been so inhibited about the inappropriateness of "acting out" behavior that we have tended to stop children from this sort of overacting. But in a sense this is the most important preliminary form for understanding character. Just as one often must throw oneself totally into a sport before one learns its more subtle maneuvers, so one must throw oneself into character in a similar fashion. This is the age where the Keystone Cops, the great comedians of action (Harold Lloyd, the Three Stooges, Abbott and Costello) and a hundred cartoon characters represent what character is all about.

In the *stage of technique* we come to the truth argued by those who believe that improvisation should be acting, not psychodrama. But, as we have argued, what they will get if they start here is shallow if intelligible performances. This approach is often advocated by those who have this professional point of view because they tend to deal only with volunteers or with students of acting rather than with the general run of children. The children they deal with have talent, and talent has a capacity to skip the stages that the rest of us must labor through.

The great modern device for developing technique is *theater games*. These are entirely appropriate for children and a lot of fun in their own way, even if we do not have acting in mind. A well-known theater game is the mirror game, in which two players act as if one is looking in a mirror and the other is the reflection in the mirror. It has the advantage that it can be played anywhere any time. It calls for considerable thought on how to make actions that the other can follow or how to concentrate sufficiently so you can mimic the other's actions.

These are really games of order, because both players are trying to overcome anarchy. They are not meant to be games of competition, which children of this age tend to make them if you do not explain to them carefully that these are games of communication. You win if the two work together perfectly. The growth of these kinds of games and their extensive use in "sensitivity" groups seems to indicate that we have a need for more collaboration and more order in our society.

In the audience game one or two players have to communicate to the others by their behavior a sport that they are observing. Tennis is the easiest. The players agree beforehand what sport they will watch, but they must make no other verbal arrangements. All the rest is done by mutual paying attention to each other. They must not communicate by words the meaning of their audience behavior either.

In another game, the "who are they?" game, one person begins by being somebody in action; when one of the watchers recognizes the role, she joins in the actions appropriately, as do others as they "get" the act. Perhaps, for example, the first person is gardening. Others will, in effect, join in the gardening; some weeding, some digging, some wheeling the barrow. An excellent source for hundreds of these games, which call the players' attention to acting as a technique (but in a playful way), is Viola Spolin's *Improvisation for the Theater*.[1]

This is not of course the end of improvisation or drama, but it is usually about as far as we will get with children

[1] Viola Spolin, *Improvisation for the Theater* (Evanston, Ill.: North-western University Press, 1963).

through the age of twelve years. There are at least two more stages that we know of, thanks to the work of our student Cornelia Brunner, but these usually occur in adolescence and then only for those who gain some sophistication in their art form. The first, stage four, is *art as feeling*. This is when the children begin themselves to see their use of realism, message, or technique as a way of conveying feeling. Here they see any art form as the use of the media for personal expression.

A final stage, *art as empathy*, involves children's knowing what the author was trying to communicate and the way in which the author did it. Here the emphasis is on conveying or appreciating the feeling that the author had in mind through the techniques that were used. It is important to know that such higher levels exist, because there are occasionally children of eleven or twelve years who reach forward to such levels. It is also important to realize that these stages are cumulative. There is always some sense in which the realistic, moralistic, technical, feeling, or empathic responses to an art form are relevant.

Creative Writing

For some children it is much easier to express their feelings through writing than through acting. Not all forms of expression are equally available to all children. Thus, while some might be acting out the scene of an accident, others can be "reporting" it. Some may want to act the play, others may prefer to write it up and edit it, some may want to illustrate it, and still others may try to add verse, song, or musical accompaniment.

The stories that children make up during childhood, like their art, go through a series of levels which provide us with an important way of understanding where they are.

At *level* 1 (5–6 years) the youngest children tell stories in which monsters threaten, accidents happen, and there is a sense of terrible things going on. But nothing is done about it. Here is an example:

> Once upon a time there was a giant monster. When he was asleep his Mommy came in. She woke him up because she wanted to tell him that dinner was ready. The giant ate the first bowl of cereal and then he ate ten more. He got so fat that he blew up the whole house.

At *level* 2 (7–8 years) the story characters begin to respond to the threat or trouble. They call for help, they hide, they run away, they laugh at the devil. But they do not really do much for themselves. For example:

> This is a story about an alley cat. He worked for a living by digging ditches. He was a very playful cat and liked to play tricks on the keeper of the building. He liked to look at the globe of the earth because he liked to dream about taking a long sailing trip. One morning he woke up to find himself on a sailing trip in the Caribbean with his mother. He met another sailing ship in the ocean that had a devil as a captain. The cat laughed when he saw the devil. He did not fear him because he knew he could bite him. The devil's pig came along and found ink and drank it. Then he turned into a dress sitting at a desk. The cat shut his eyes when he saw this and rubbed his magic ring. He woke up and found he was having a dream and it was all done.

At *level* 3 (9–10 years) the story characters begin to be successful in reacting to the danger or threat. They safeguard themselves effectively even if they do not finally remove the danger. Perhaps more importantly the storyteller can move up and down in the story, exhibiting both defeat and victory as in the adventures of Harold Hoot the Owl. There are three episodes.

1. *Mr Hoot and the Married Lady*

One night Mr Hoot was sitting in his house thinking why he never had any fun. He said to himself, "Maybe I'm too shy" So he said to himself again that he was going to go out and get into mischief. He got on his coat and put on his contact lenses and he was off.

There he was strolling from bar to bar. At his fifth bar, be dicided to have a drink. He pounded on the table and said two martinis on the rocks. While he was waiting for his two drinks, he took off his shoes and socks and picked his feet. Then he got his drinks and chug-a-lugged them down the hatch. After his drinks, he saw a beautiful lady in the corner of the bar. So he went over to her and said "Can I buy you a drink." She replied "No thank you. I'm not finished with this one." Then she said "Anyway please sit down and we will talk".

A big guy walking out of the mens room came over to Mr Hoot and said "Are you fooling around with my wife?" How dare you" and picked Mr Hoot up and threw him on the ground. The moral of the story is—you can't tell a married lady from a single lady.

2. *Mr Hoot and the Stewardess*

Once Mr Hoot was sitting in the bar with his friend Bobby the Baboon. They were discussing going to Hollywood. Mr Hoot said to Bobby lets go next week. So they made all the arrangements and before they knew it they were on the airplane going to

Hollywood. While they were on the airplane, Mr Hoot saw this very atractive stewardess. So Mr. Hoot called her over and said "Hi what's your name?" She said "Laura Sinch," "whats yours"? "Harold Hoot, He said. Then he said, "How long have you been working for the airlines." She replied, "Two years and seven months. Then they started talking about where they lived and other things like that. Then a little baboon said, "Hey would you stop it with the lady and let her do what she's supposed to be doing." Then Harold got mad and said "Shut up you little baboon." Then Bobby said, "Hey are you sounding on my kind "How dare you." Oh Bobby but out of this Harold replied. Then the little baboon said "Shut up you overgrown owl." Then they really started going at it. They were throwing pillows and suitcases at each other and cursing at each other. Then Harold gave him a good sock in the face and that was the end of that adventure.

In level 4 (11–12 years) we get the conventional hero or fairy tale ending. The hero wins out and not only beats out the bad guy but takes over the kingdom and there can be no more threat.

It seems that all children normally go through some such series as this between the ages of five and twelve years if they are free to do so. They undoubtedly do it in their daydreams even if they cannot reach for it in their stories. It is probably very important for them to have this other storytelling avenue also. When a school system is free enough to let children tell stories in this way they can also grow through their stories. They can be regressive in them (Mr Hoot, episode 1) or progressive in them (Mr Hoot episode 2), and they can end up with a rosy ending as in the following final episode in the story of Mr Hoot:

3. Mr Hoot gets married

Once Harold was sitting in a restaurant at a table all by himself. Then he noticed there was a female owl sitting down by herself. Mischievously he walked over and asked her what her name was. She said, Mary Gline" Then Harold thought for a moment and said, "Are you the girl that broke her wing when you were nine years old?" Then she said, "What's your name and how did you know about my wing?" "Well said Harold I knew about your wing because your name sounded very familiar so I thought back to my childhood and remembered that a girl named Mary broke her wing, and my name is Harold Hoot" Then she said "You were the kid they called Hoot the Toot "Oh yeh Harold replied, "I forgot about that." Then they started to talk about their childhood and ate dinner together.

After that night they went out to dinner, to movies and did lots of other things like that. After about a year they told their parents they were going to get married. Their parents agreed and they had a wedding. They had the most beautiful wedding you could imagine. For their honeymoon they went to Niagara Falls. Then after that they settled down in a nice house in poughkeepsie and had to boys named Bobby and Peter. Last and not least—lived happily ever after.

As a child does not normally become aware of himself as a self ("I am me!") until about nine or ten years, stories like play are one of the ways in which he tries out who he is; one of the ways of being a self. We can tell something of a child's flexibility by his flexibility in these stories. Is he flexible in them, or does he always tell rather routine stereotyped tales?

In most schools the teaching of stories is so stereotyped that we cannot answer this question. Teachers show the children just how to compose a story and expect them to copy set models. As a result stories are no longer a place where the children can play, which means they are no longer a place for very personal growth.

Where story writing is a freely encouraged activity we can see the child gradually building a narrative plot in his head. The first stories are simple actions or climaxes. The final ones have characters and plot. Probably each child has to build such soap operas in his head, before he can really grasp them in the films and television as they are presented to him. Usually children under nine and ten do not retell a very coherent tale after they have seen or heard it. Our argument would be that they cannot do this because they haven't constructed the counterpart in their own heads. Playfulness allows the growth of these internal soap operas.

Of course, it is more serious than that. The internal narrative also allows the understanding of legend and mythology and all the patriotic stories which we try to tell them. When we talk about children being able to tell and therefore understand stories we are talking about the origin or genesis of mythology. In children's stories as in the myths of the world, the heroes come to a fate that can be judged by the same four levels above. It is no small insult, we believe, when parents or teachers interfere with the maximum flexible growth of this internal narrative, on the grounds that they are teaching sentences or paragraphs. On such trivial grounds we make it difficult for children to develop their own capacity for myth making, which is what writing stories, novels, and plays is all about.

The big shifts that occur in *verse* from the earlier age periods to this one are as follows. Up until about nine children are very much affected by sounds in language, more often than they respond to sense. This is why they are inclined to see poetry only as a matter of rhyme or to like the many "sounding" nonsense rhymes of childhood:

> Hibberty, Bibberty, I Saliberty,
> Pompalary Jig,
> Every man who has no hair,
> Ought to wear a wig.

It is said that the four-year-old John Keats went about providing rhymes in response to anything said to him. Younger children also have a shorter memory span and consequently prefer shorter lengths to their verses. The following is an old counting-out rhyme used by eight-year-olds that is for them also high poetry:

> First grade, baby,
> Second grade, tot,
> Third grade, angel,
> Fourth grade, snot.

It is not hard to remember the following verses:

> There was an old woman
> And her name was Pat,
> And when she died,
> She did like *that*.

> Pig snout
> Walk out.

Another childish feature of verse is the use of a series of numbers or letters, which children already know well and can use as a memory device to handle a larger amount of information;

thus, "What's the initial of my sweetheart? A. B. C. D. . . ." or "Ten little, nine little, eight little indians. . . ."

Children's thinking also tends not to be as systematic as it is habitual. Thus, for example, if they are given the word "red" and asked to tell you what it makes them think of next, the next word they give you will probably be "apple" (as in red apple) or "rose" (as in red rose). Older children of ten are as likely to respond with another color, such as "green," or with the word "color" itself. Older children thus give you a classification of the word you have given them, whereas younger children give you a response to which they have become accustomed. One idea leads by association to another:

> I went downtown
> To see Mrs. Brown.
> She gave me a nickel
> To buy a pickle.
> The pickle was sour,
> She gave me a flower.
> The flower was dead,
> She gave me a thread.
> The thread was thin,
> She gave me a pin.
> The pin was sharp,
> She gave me a harp.
> The harp began to sing
> Minnie and a minnie and a ha, ha, ha.

Increasingly from the age of eight onward children become interested in the relationships between meaning rather than those between sounds. The riddles of the last chapter and the verse with which that chapter ended ("I come before you to stand behind you . . .") both make a joke out of changing meanings. Usually by eleven years of age the types or rhyme that we have listed above are of little interest to children.

They seem too babyish to them. Where simple rhymes occur, they begin to feature social commentary and violations of moral decor, such as obscenities:

> Violets are blue
> And I turned red
> As soon as I saw you
> Nude in bed.

> Jesus loves me, this I know,
> For the bible tells me so,
> I am Jesus little lamb
> My bloody oath I am.

From a creative point of view children at this time prefer to invest themselves in prose poems rather than in rhyming verses. Thus, although we might advocate sounding and rhyming madnesses, alliterations, and the like for younger children, we now focus attention on what is to be said. Arranging a series of thoughts in order is sometimes a more profitable approach to verse at eleven years than is thinking in terms of poetic structure.

The same focus is important in story writing. We should emphasize what children care about, and all the remarks made above about improvisations and art apply again here. Sometimes story writing can be prompted when children write a "novel." To make their own first book is exciting to the fifth graders, particularly if they can make drawings and cartoons to go with it. Making up stories orally always helps. This can be around the dinner table, in the car, or in the classroom. One person starts off. Others have to pick up the story where the first one leaves off. Usually they leave the hero in dire straits, and some fancy extrication is necessary for the following person.

Game Simulation

Nine through twelve years is a time of great enthusiasm for games, an enthusiasm that has been fully seized upon in education only in recent years. In *The Study of Games* we have written extensively about the use of games for teaching purposes first by the armies of the world in the eighteenth century and then by business education in this century.[2] It appears that children can learn as much through games as they learn in more-ordinary ways, and they have a much higher motivation when doing so.

As a result of this, there are now innumerable game curricula in which parents and teachers attempt to get their children reading, doing arithmetic, and so forth through games. A good example is the recent book by J. H. Humphrey and Dorothy D. Sullivan called *Teaching Slow Learners through Active Games*.[3] There are also many companies that market *game simulations*. These are attempts to teach everything from economics to history through a game. Usually game simulations, unlike real games, are good for only a few lessons, after which all the tricks have been learned and one must move on to another gamelike lesson.[4]

What all this means is that our old attitudes about games' being trivial and of no account were apparently wrong. Throughout human history different cultures have used different games to teach what had to be known. Games were the first schools. Games of strategy (checkers, chess) arose in human history with the rise of systematic social-class distinctions and the rise of warrior classes. They were ways of

[2] Eliot Avedon and Brian Sutton-Smith, *The Study of Games* (New York: John Wiley & Sons, 1971).

[3] J. H. Humphrey and Dorothy D. Sullivan, *Teaching Slow Learners through Active Games* (Springfield, Ill.: Charles C. Thomas, 1970).

[4] There is even a newspaper called *Simulation Gaming News,* which is published at Stanford University.

teaching strategic thinking to beginners and for keeping diplomats and military men in a state of preparation. Likewise, games of chance arose where divination and magic were ways of attempting to influence the gods. Games of physical skill arose where there was a need to practice the arts of hunting and gathering.[5]

We are not going to list here all the games to play with children. There are too many, and they are well documented elsewhere. Perhaps we should say that just as there are personality differences, so there are differences in the way parents like to be playful with children, which means that not all parents who want to be playful will want to play games, just as not all will want to improvise or to talk about dreams.

These are just different media that will be used by different kinds of parents. Some parents do all their play through witty conversation, for example, and that is it; that is all they do. We had to point this out here because in a book on play it might seem that games would be orthodox. They are not. Games are only one of the ways in which people get to be playful with each other. Like all the other ways people can be a bore in games just as they can elsewhere. Some playful people find games boring!

Games are usually fun for children, even if they are not your cup of tea. Almost anything can be made acceptable at this age if it can be turned into a game. Note that in this respect children's tolerance for games lasts longer than does their tolerance for fantasy, which tends to fade around ten years. Games are at a high peak at least through fifteen years. A particularly "playful" use of this mania for games is to have your children construct them. In this way the parallel urge for technical craft competency and interest in the games themselves both get scope.

[5] The reader who is interested in this kind of anthropological material will find more details in our book *The Folkgames of Children* (Austin, Tex.: University of Texas Press, 1973).

Naturally, the most interesting constructions are of Monopoly-type games, where the game can be converted to quite different uses and children can have fun making the boards, and the like. For example, one game expert, Bernard de Koven, has suggested that Monopoly could be renamed Treaty and stand for two countries negotiating for peace. Then the Chance and Community Chest cards would have to be rewritten to include "Your ambassador has a cold. Go back three spaces." The playing pieces become doves and hawks. Dollars become bombs.

Still, the idea is not just to do this or that but to play the game a lot and then have a playful time arguing about the changes you would like and why you would introduce them. In this way you become your own game simulators. It seems advisable to begin this with one of the well-known race games like Monopoly (the players are competing to see who gets to a certain goal first). With experience, however, it becomes possible to make a comparative survey of some of the other favorite games with a discussion of their techniques. To what extent are they different? How do Ludo or Chutes and Ladders differ from checkers or chess? What are the combinations of pure chance, shrewd guessing, and strategy (we define strategy as rational decision making)?

This playful game simulation is of incredible promise because the games are models of almost everything we do in human life; for example, an examination of the games with sophisticated eleven- and twelve-year-olds takes you into social science and politics. We have argued that games are models of power in human history and that they are ways of teaching the techniques of power to those who play them.[6]

In the simple abstract of games people could learn these techniques without the dangers that usually ensue if they tried out their power in a real situation. Without a knowl-

---

[6] See, for example, Sutton-Smith, B., and Rosenberg, B. S., *The Sibling* (New York: Holt, Rinehart & Winston, 1971) chap. 4.

edge of power tactics (deception, decision making, bribery, feinting, blackmail) how could anyone possibly succeed in business, war, politics, and even marriage? One must know these things even if only to defend oneself against them. Yet we do not teach them explicitly in school. We leave the study of power to children themselves and to the playground, as we have seen in prior chapters.

More can be done than that. Constructing games and discussing what goes into them are the kind of practical activity that leads to questions about the whys and wherefores of human behavior with this age group. Begin at age nine with the simplest chance games, where the rolls of dice take the children through different territories. Here the fun is in moving through the territories and being sent back so many spaces or whatever. Then move on to the addition of strategic exchanges, such as in the game of Monopoly. After that there is chess; in the future, the presidency?

The Sandlot Sport

Nothing angers some people more than whether children of this age should be playing little league baseball or pony football. Many adults see in it a travesty of adult-child relationships. They argue that the children become pawns in the parents' concern for victory. The coaches play with the youngsters like checkers on a board. As a result there is not much real fun for the children, and often, as soon as they get into adolescence, they drop these games forever. This is one side of the picture.

Other parents argue that their children love these sports. They love the uniforms. They love having such well-organized competition. These parents say that without these games their children would have nothing to do (nor would the parents). The alternative is just more television or more

horsing around in dangerous streets. With such divided opin-
ions we are clearly talking to different parents with different
life styles. There are some parents who can suggest plenty of
alternative activities for their children. There are some parents
who have few.

This conflict is similar to the one about whether high
school athletics helps or hinders academic progress. The evidence shows that for an upper-income boy it is a hindrance.
Upper-income achievers tend to play individual games (tennis, golf, etc.) rather than team games. But for lower socio-
economic team players, their grades rise. Team games contribute character formation of an orthodox nature to those
who are not used to it. They are not of great value to those
who can take such character formation for granted.

A similar situation occurs in the T-shirt leagues of this
country. For children whose parents have been rising in social
status, T-shirt leagues represent an organized experience of
team activity. This was not a part of the gang activity to
which their parents may have been formerly accustomed. Although these leagues may not be well conducted nor ideal in
themselves, they are associated with the kind of status for
which such people are striving. One has to find a substitute,
not merely deplore the form.

The substitute is, of course, some form of sandlot provi-
sion. Many adults would not oppose little leagues if they con-
sisted of games in which teams were picked out for each
occasion on home ground and did not require too much apparatus and costuming. If adults would be willing to give their
voluntary supervision to such informal events, staged at
regular times on local grounds, all the legitimate purposes
would be served as far as preadolescence was concerned. This
would not, of course, preclude competition between areas in
the same townships toward the end of a season.

What has to occur, however, is the making of such provi-
sions not only for children but also for people of all ages who

are not linked into the fairly professional streams that begin to affect children when they get into high school. There is a need for sandlot games for those over thirty and forty as much as for those under ten. A healthy community would seek to build an informal sports organization for members of all age levels rather than for just one age level. It is more likely that under these circumstances better supervision and better sponsorship of play for the young would occur, because the parents would be proceeding with a concern for total community health rather than just the willingness of a few parents who aspire to be coaches and to force their young charges along a quasi-professional path.

In the *sandlot principle* play and sports both meet and part company. Where the group is one of acquaintances who know each other well, allowances are made (by handicapping) for age and skill differences. The major concern is a good game on a particular afternoon. It may require some elder statesmen or "coaches" to pick the teams on each occasion. The aim of these elders is to get a drawn match by their skill at selection, or it may just emerge from the alternating choices of two leaders. But however chosen, the aim is a match of skill. Without that match attention and interest wane.

The value of the small game or small sport of this kind is that if it engages attention, it recharges the battery of the participants. All we know both anthropologically and psychologically about sports is that they reproduce the desires and attitudes of the culture in which they are played. There is exhibition of skill, courage, achievement, and the like, but all these traits can be displayed here without the usual complexities of ordinary living. The usual harassments and ambiguities are gone.

In the game we take out these drives and give them a quick and clean production. We commit ourselves in a thoroughly self-concerned way to a demonstration of our skill. We focus our attention totally on the limited field and get an unambiguous feedback. As a result, we come up out of a good game with our ambitions revamped and our usual attitudes retinged with optimism. Games regenerate us.

It is this, we think, that underlies the constant concern of many people that children should be taught to play for the game's sake rather than for winning. To play just to win is to sacrifice this life-sustaining value that truly playful indulgence can bring. Of course it is seldom that one does either one or the other. What is necessary is engrossment in the game itself, and that the engrossment be attached to ways of gaming that can last throughout the adult years, when they are often most needed. The professionalization of sports in the young is no help to the middle-aged, who would have been better off if introduced to a sandlot principle they could continue as the years went by.

Playfulness and Creativity

Sometimes it may be difficult to decide whether we are advocating playfulness or creativity. That is because playfulness and creativity are interrelated. There is experimental evidence that shows that when children are trained to be more imaginative, by having an adult play imaginatively with them over a period of time, their scores on independent creativity tests also increase.

Being playful, which means doing novel things for the fun of it, may not be too much different from doing novel things because you want to. Usually when we ask children to give us unique answers (what are all the things you can think of to do with a pencil?), their first responses are pretty conventional (draw, write), but as time goes by, they get more unique (make a candy apple stick, balance it on my nose). Similarly, when children explore something, they are at first pretty careful, and their responses are appropriate to the object; as time passes, however, they begin to introduce more novelty. They get more playful. Both creativity and play, therefore, require a considerable period of habitual response before they usually come into action. In that they are quite similar. They are responses that come late in the human repertoire.

But although they have novelty in common, creativity, like work, is more purposive and intent than is play. Play need not produce novelty. It can be idle, be offhand, and be repetitious. Play is more subjective. It produces its novelty as much by willfulness as by intent. What we think happens is that through play children incidentally produce much novelty, which is then available to them at a later time if and when they should be called upon to make creative responses. Play provides the repertoire of novelty that creativity uses.

THE CHILD'S OWN PLAY

We do not think of children "playing" solitarily in this age period. But of course in their manifold model construction, collections, hobbies, crafts, and even reading they are often almost as much at play as they were at an earlier stage with blocks. The play is masked beneath the excuse that this is a construction of some sort. But during the process of the building and the making the activity is often immersed in emerging daydreams and must be reckoned as play. Not unnaturally, the daydreams are of a potential future when the players are the flyers of the airplane model they are constructing or the beauty behind the miniature doll whose fashions they are busily displaying. With one or more companions the same loose web of daydream and reality may wind around their performance of musical instruments together or dancing to the record player.

Occasionally children of this age will continue to play out

their fantasies with more elaborate imitative play than they were capable of when younger. We have seen ten- and eleven-year-old boys engaging in elaborate imaginative space games with very few properties and much complex discussion, following very closely the type of discourse picked up from the various moon shots. This is not solitary play, but it is a more sophisticated form of the first informal group play that we noticed as early as four years. Girls, in the same fashion, may imagine themselves as doctors, lawyers, and teachers.

Although the content of this informal play represents the preoccupations that the men and women of a particular culture might have, what is most important is that the level of imaginative complexity in social behavior is probably greater than is that to be found anywhere else in these children's behavior, at least at a level they can maintain spontaneously without the help of elders.

Another feature of informal play at this time is its *secrecy*. This is an age when children realize they are mentally free of adults. It is about nine years of age or so that children sometimes report their first "I am me" experience—the experience of being a person in their own right, with their own mind and their own thoughts.

Much of the peer activity of nine- through twelve-year-olds is discovering that there are others who share the same feelings and that one is not alone in being a nine- or ten-year-old self. One way to validate oneself is through endless conversations with other selves. They find out what they are like and what others are like. Another way to validate oneself is through endless actions with other selves. They discover what they can do and what others can do. Both the talking and the actions reveal the self, show that one is like others, and lead to acceptance by others.

Furthermore, they have in common that they are mentally free of adults, and children have to explore that new freedom also. Often they symbolize the new freedom physically by having a fort or some special hideaway under the house, in the basement, or in the woods; or they adopt one of the many gibberish languages that enable them to communicate secretly, even if at great length, in the presence of others, although they are often more concerned with the power of the idea of secrecy rather than with its use. Parents who can occasionally contribute the rules of secret languages are useful to have around.

Formal Games

In general, the concern with technique in art and crafts and with construction in play becomes a concern with skill in games. The two prior stages give way in this stage to a focus on individual skill. One's position is now maintained in a game not by any magically given powers, as when one is chosen to be "It" by some counting-out rhyme; now one usually gets and maintains one's position only by competence.

Competition with other players, however, is still by and large fairly indirect. Seldom does one player face up to another player alone (as in boxing and wrestling). Competition takes place among numbers of players, each playing for himself or each occasionally or usually cooperating with others. This reduces the intensity of the contest and makes its more difficult and dangerous aspects more easily assimilable. There is also a beginning of team games, although only in the sense of two packs or mobs contesting against each other. It is too early yet for specialized team games in children's spontaneous play.

Chasing and Escaping

In all the earlier forms of chasing and escaping we dealt essentially with one individual against the others. Now we begin to see at least temporary groups forming. Some of the new games of chasing and escaping that nine- to ten-year-olds play follow.

In Red Rover the player who is "It" in the center calls the other players to come across one at a time. If she catches them, they join her in the center and help her catch the others. If one player runs across from base to base, all players are entitled to run across. She may have to tag the running player, to drag him down to the ground, or to "crown" him. In the latter case she holds her hand on the other player's head, crying out some words such as "One-two-three-Sinio" or "King Caeser, one two, three." In "kinging" the captured player has to be held on the ground while patted on the head. The last player caught calls the next player across. Should a player succeed in crossing, that player calls out "All over" or "Pass over," and the rest run across, as many as are then caught taking their place in the middle. Naturally, the first child called is usually the weakest runner. Under many different names this game is the most widespread and popular game of children of this age level.

There are also various games in which those who are discovered join the seeker in looking for the rest or in which one person hides and, when he is discovered, he is joined by the seekers, one at a time, so that the last person to discover him becomes "It" next time. (Sardines is the usual name of this game.) Sometimes intensity is added to these games in a special way. Thus, although ball tag is the same game as the chasing or tagging of the earlier age, the players here tag by throwing a ball at each other, particularly a wet ball, which means that it can hurt.

In these games we can see the momentary appearance of a team relationship, as in Red Rover, where in the middle of the game the number of players in the middle approximately equals the number at the end bases. Here are, in effect, two contending sides of transitory, yet organized, nature. Similarly, in sardines at one point half the players are hidden and half are still searchers. In Red Rover the teamsmanship is parallel. All have the same aim in view but do not interrelate with each other in any more fundamental way than that. There is momentary role differentiation within the middle team insofar as each latest-caught player gets to call the next one across, so that for the moment that player is the leader. Both team relationships and leadership are thus transitory at this level.

Another important change in role relationships is the increasing focus on the individual player who can withstand all the rest. This is not now the harassed central player, as at the previous age level, but is another individual who in the course of Red Rover or hide and seek becomes the last individual left whom all the rest of the players either try to catch or to find. In Red Rover that player is often the best runner or the strongest player, who has been able to fend off the other players throughout the course of the game. At the end, however, they gang up against her and drag her to the ground, showing their best collaboration in that final moment of the game.

The hiding, chasing, and capturing remain in these games, but the *acts* have increased in forcefulness. There is less symbolic action associated with the performance (tagging) and more out and out direct physical contact in the grabbing hold of the runner and slapping him on the back of the head three times. Mothers speak of Red Rover as the "clothes-tearing" game, and it is often temporarily halted in the playground as a result of their outcries. Although we want to emphasize the increase in direct testing of each other, it is important to note that this testing is momentary rather than continuous, as will become the case at the next level.

With the two bases at each end and most of the action taking place between them, the bases take on a more neutral and less dynamic quality than in the previous age levels. Whereas at the previous age levels the bases are in a sense the goals of the game (to hide in a safe space, to return to the den or home base, to hold one's prisoners), at this level bases serve more as conventional instruments to the action taking place between them. Perhaps this is symbolized by the shift to a rectangular playing field from a mainly radial or circular one. (At the two previous levels, the players radiated out from some central base or circled around it.) The game has moved from bases and safe spaces to action over territory within *boundaries* at the sides and at both ends. Some would say children have moved from a sacred to a profane definition of space.

More *plot* exists in these games also, instead of just a series of episodes. The plot "thickens" as it extends over time. There is indeed a sense of *climax* among the players as they make the final efforts to pull down the most powerful remaining player who has succeeded in running through the middle on all other occasions. There are more evidences of their whispering together and of their ganging up on the final runner.

We can sum up the different uses of time in games from age five through twelve as follows. Time in the games of five- and six-year-olds is largely episodic. Each piece of the game succeeds each other, as in games of tag, without any larger organization. The game can break off at the end of any piece with no consequences. We can call this episodic time. In novels we call it picaresque: one thing leads to another; a series of events are chained together, but there is no larger plot.

In the games of seven- and eight-year-olds, however, we begin to see a joining of the episodes into a larger structure. In the game of ringolevio, release, or kick the can the player who is "It" must capture all the players one after the other until they are all accumulated in the base; then and only then can we say that phase of the game is over. This is also true of ring games, such as "The Farmer in the Dell." The episodes are strung together, and although similar in nature, they add up cumulatively to the final phase, when everyone pinches the cheese. We can call this *cumulative* time. Seven-year-olds have a more complex sense of play time than do five-year-olds. There are folktales that also have this cumulative character, like "Henny Penny."

By nine and ten years of age we have added, at least momentarily, *climax* time. In the game of Red Rover there are moments when everyone is after the strongest player. This is a climax. This is even more true of king of the castle, when after a series of efforts the many players manage to drag down the strongest. By the age of twelve and the emergence of sports, of course, time gets arranged into regular periods and can be called *interval* time. In those cases the time within the regular period is still at times episodic (one down in football), cumulative (three downs), or climactic (a touchdown). Modern football's invention of *elastic time* is something else.

At about eleven or twelve years we are ready for the final childhood stage in games of chasing and escaping, when the two teams become fixed in nature to start with, although they may attempt to capture players from the other side as the game proceeds. Hares and hounds, paperchase, or prisoner's base are games of this kind. In hares and hounds one group pursues another over a great distance. These major games of twelve-year-olds in days gone by were practiced as various forms of pursuit and combat. Usually there was little clear leadership or specialization in positions (as there is in baseball, for example). On a childhood level they are like the mob games that used to be played in the Middle Ages, when two separate villages would vie for the possession of a ball at a festival once a year.

When playing group games with children, it is probably easier and more fun when the teams are of this relatively diffuse variety and the positions are not particularly specialized. In this way everyone gets experience in doing everything. Later in adolescence sufficient differences emerge in the skill of the players, and games may not proceed well without allowing for the specialists.

The subsequent history of chasing and escaping in games is to be found in baseball players' running around the bases or football players' running for a touchdown pursued by the opposition. It is surprising that this theme in human relationships, which we saw begin one-sidedly at the end of the first year of life, continues to excite us even in adult years. If our argument is correct, we never quite overcome our feeling that we have to be alert to matters of this kind.

Success and Failure

Younger children were concerned with being correct and not making mistakes. More and more at this age level the issue becomes winning and losing because of the more direct confrontation between players. By ten years of age players are more ready to win and lose. The outcomes of the game are clear-cut. Today this tends to take place with the use of the ball in some form as the agency (baseball or football), although in former times (and in some places still) marbles, tops, hoops, buttons, knives, stones, and coins were the center of the action. If we focus on actions rather than on agencies of play, then there are games in which running, hopping, jumping, throwing, hitting, pitching, and dexterity are the central issue.

What tends to happen between the age of nine and twelve years is that the confrontations from player to player get more direct and the force and danger of the actions that they carry out become more severe. Often there is no change in the structure of the game (from tag to ball tag), but its dangers increase tremendously. The organization of mumbly peg was not very different from jacks, but played with a knife its consequences for cut hands were very different.

Because ours is an information culture, success these days is scored as often through items of information as through moments of physical prowess. Each of the following games usually capitalizes on the mastery of some intellectual skill that is reaching ripeness at the time the game seems most appropriate for the participants. Some games evoke reasoning and classificatory ability, as does twenty questions (which is also one of the most useful of automobile games). There are *memory* games, in which each player must retain everything already mentioned by every other player. There are *decoding* games, involving initials, alphabets, anagrams, and classes of things; *observation* games; *number* games (buzz); and *vocabulary* games (Scrabble).

Attack and Defense

The fantasy of attack and defense begins in games of cowboys or witches. By the age of nine it is often hard to tell whether the main aim of a game is chasing and escaping, success or failure, or attack and defense. It is partly a matter of how hard the players are handled. If players are punched as they run across the middle in Red Rover, is that pursuit or attack? Still, this age involves games where attack and defense become central, as in king of the mountain and dodge ball, in which everyone attacks the central player and she for her part attempts to hold her position against all attackers. There are also various forms of rough and tumble or wrestling, which become increasingly popular during this period, as strong players become more ready to engage in direct attack and defense.

Probably, however, most of such attack and defense occurs

indirectly, as in games of success and failure, where one attacks the opponent's marbles or tops, or in baseball, where one pitches the player out with strike three rather than hitting him directly. In football, of course, both attack and pursuit are combined with high intensity. In games of *strategy*, such as checkers and chess, which become popular at these ages, the attack is also indirect via the chessmen. But to some this indirect means of attack is even more devastating than is direct physical attack, particularly in an age like our own, where mental power and decision making (rather than physical prowess) have become much more central to both our economic and our cultural survival. It can feel worse to be mentally wiped out than to be tackled physically.

With these games occasional participation and occasional example seem to be the best way for parents to contribute. Children need information, and they need skill. The right games introduced at the right age can endow children with a technique both for their own intellectual and physical development and for that interaction with others that is most sought after throughout childhood.

EPILOGUE

Put simply, we have argued that the family that plays together stays together—and laughs together and generally celebrates each others' existence together. If we admit that families are going to be fewer and smaller, it makes sense to realize that child rearing and parent rearing may become a highly specialized and precious activity. It has always been a difficult thing to do anyway. The hazards of raising a group of adequate human beings, although they have not been glossed over in the past, are being positively gloated over now.

For now we can choose to be a family. We can choose to

have our children. The highest achievement of parenthood should be that as our children reach adulthood, they would choose to have *us* as parents. We have a better chance of this happening if for twenty-odd years we have all lived together in an atmosphere that has been full of playfulness and fun. By playing with your children, you as the parents can turn the roles of life around the other way. *You* or they can be the clowns, horses, babies, monsters, the ones who are "It," and the tricksters. Your children feel comfortable with you because you can change places with them and they can change with you. It is an optimistic and lighthearted way of life to be able to go back and forth from the way things really are to the way things might be.

But as we have said all along, there are times *not to play* with your children—not ever *if* you feel you are intruding (and you may be), or you feel it is a duty (for their "own good"), or you are too grumpy, preoccupied, or just plain exhausted to enjoy the fun you are supposed to be having together. By and large as children get older, we have to play with them less, but we have to understand them more. At an earlier age they are so dependent upon us that they come to us with their play. At these later ages they do not, and we have to have a wiser understanding of what they are about in order to be of occasional help.

12 | Conclusion

Primarily we hope that we have made the world more fun or at least a less boring place for you and your children. We believe, however, that we have also contributed to your versatility, and to your children's versatility, because they will copy you, whatever you do.

ASSESSMENT

The appendix at the end of this book, which we call "Assessment," is divided into two parts. The first part contains a check list that you can use to review *your own progress* in these things. It asks you, in effect, how playful you have been and how playful you think that you can become. Is it too embarrassing to be this childish? Both religious leaders and psychologists have often indicated that the truly mature person has the capacity to be both childlike and playful when it is desirable. Creativity encompasses the ability to reproduce in play all the stages of one's life. Fortunately with young children a parent can approach this gradually. Children are enormously cooperative in such efforts. Fun beckons in its own way and shapes us all toward its mutual enjoyment, unless we are determined to withstand it.

The second part contains a check list that outlines the *children's progress* through the various forms of play that we have discussed in earlier chapters. This list serves as the *grammar* of their play and games. It outlines the building blocks through which children will normally proceed. Although it is only a primitive map, it is at least a starting point or base line for your understanding. The learning of play and games is not simply the learning of actions; it is also the learning of emotional dynamics like surprise, anticipation, and climax. All of this learning comes about in a systematic way.

THEORY OF PLAY

But now we come to the very difficult question of what it is we are talking about. What is play? What is a game? Although we have dropped hints here and there on our thinking, by and large we have felt that, practically speaking, it is possible both to play and to see play's effects without necessarily knowing how it works. One can often carry something out very effectively without theoretical knowledge. Nevertheless, living intelligently requires at least an effort at understanding what it is we are about.

Play is a subject about which a great deal has been written, but on which there is as yet little science. After all, we all play to some extent and therefore imagine ourselves to be authorities. To discuss play adequately we have to say something about our *motives*, our *feelings*, and our *thoughts*.

The Motive for Play—a Reversal of Power

Play is one type of voluntary behavior—that is, a behavior undertaken because people want to do something, not because they must do it. They are motivated from within. Unlike other kinds of voluntary activity, where behavior is partly controlled by objects and other people, in play the players are even freer in their choices of action. Many theorists have written that people play because of the pleasure of being the cause of what is happening. This is the pleasure of being in power.

We have noted the many occasions where it is possible to

argue that in play or games the players reverse the way things usually are. They make things happen their way rather than the way they usually happen. Instead of being frightened by monsters, they become the monster themselves. In the game of "Moonlight, Starlight, Bogey Won't Come Out Tonight," played at twilight, the children who are "It" become themselves the frightening creatures. Even when they are running from the person who is "It," they control the circumstances because they can hide, they can run, or if they wish, they can simply call the game off.

They get to deal with the dangers and uncertainties in this situation in a way that is within their control, and if they feel they are losing control, then they stop playing the game. Either way they are safe, yet they can have the excitement of dealing with such real issues as being pursued by dangerous creatures. In most of our lives we do not have such control. If we are children, we have even less of it.

The activities of infants in their very first month of play—when they blow bubbles on their lips in a relaxed manner—suggest the first reversal of the flow of events. For the first time the human subjects have stepped away from those things that impel them (hunger, pain, sleep) and are taking charge themselves. Since this happens so early in the first two months and since it is the first example of such self-control, we can argue that one first discovers oneself through play. Here is the first awareness of the self as being able to initiate things, as being able to control the flow of circumstances. Of course, the control exercised in play is only a fiction of what it is like to control everyday circumstances. But it is at least an experience of what the whole pattern of being in control is like. How else could one ever get the opportunity when so young?

What enters into play are those matters that we cannot control. In the young these are usually issues having to do with parents and their authority. As we get older, the issues of success and failure and life and death become the more persistent matters over which we may seek such a reversal of power.

The Feeling of Play—Viving

We have known for a long time that children do not generally play except in familiar situations with familiar people. For that matter, they do not play at unfamiliar things. Usually the actions in play reflect their own lives and those of people about them. There is enormous repetition of everyday themes—washing, eating, dressing, going to work. All of this means that they do not play unless they are quite secure. When life is too demanding, dangerous, or anxiety producing, there is no room for play. It is only when children can take the rest of life for granted and be somewhat relaxed about it that play can begin. Without such relaxation there cannot be the transition to play.

But as soon as play begins, its subject matter becomes vivid to all its participants. Even though the subject matter of play can be as diverse as playing house, chasing, or football, all players report being highly involved in their play. They also look as though they are highly engrossed. The feeling quality of play is that it is a vivid life experience. Unlike everyday affairs, which are often stressful, boring, or so-so, play is vivid. This is as true for children as it is for the spectators glued to their television sets watching their favorite forms of sport. All have in common this feeling of life's being made more vivid. We can call this vivification if we wish, but it is easier to refer to it more simply as having a *vive*.

We play and we practice sport because we want to vive, to live vividly. In those societies and historical times when people were under the pressures of famine, poverty, or war, they had much less time for this. Life was vivid enough in its own stressful way. As children and adults have become more secure in their childhood and more affluent in their society, they have sought once again to restore such vividness, but under their own control, and play is the most universal way of doing so. The search for vivid living through play, games, and sports has become an obsession of modern man. It is almost as universal a phenomenon in all major countries as the church was in the Middle Ages. Sport is modern man's ritual of the chosen life.

We may ask how this vividness is produced. It is produced by centering all attention on those things that we can control. We are not forced to pay attention to many different things. We do not have to be self-conscious about our worldly selves and all the myriad passing events and irritations of everyday life. We focus on only a small area—the play area, the sports field, the checkers board. This gives us immediate feedback. Each of our actions is meaningful in this play area. Each action has a payoff. A good move leads to the advance of one's checkers, a poor move leads to a loss. It is all very clear, although it is excitingly uncertain from moment to moment.

The fear of loss, the hope for victory, and the struggle to boss the other players in order to carry out our fantasies keep us glued into the field of action. Our feelings and the objects outside ourselves are as one. Children turn wooden blocks into their feelings of an automobile; tennis players must *feel* the flight of the ball if they are to react adequately. Play obliterates detachment and all the forms of objectivity with which we mark the path to scientific wisdom. It asks people to put their whole ego into it. Within the rules they are expected to plunge in wholeheartedly. This state of mind produces the feeling of living vividly. After the game is over, we report that it was fun. Fun apparently is a reaction to the feeling of viving.

Play as Thought—a Unique Abstraction

We do not play at everything. We only reproduce salient matters. Children playing house may run through a day's activity in ten minutes. They reproduce only certain salient characteristics of getting dressed, cleaning, eating, and going to bed. Their play is a summary, or an abstract, of their life, not its complete reproduction. The sportsmen engaged in a struggle for victory do not reproduce the struggles as they exist in life. On the contrary, in life success is seldom clear-cut. We go into business, we get married, we engage in war, and who can ever say when success or failure comes.

But in a game we have a capsule version of such a struggle. There is focus on just the struggle itself, and the outcome is clear-cut. The spatial arrangements of the playing field, the time limits under which the game takes place, and so forth, all contribute to condensing or clarifying the issue that is at stake. We speak of play as an abstract because it *removes* us from the original situation. It deals only with *general* characteristics and is a *summary* of events.

The speed at which play and games run through their reproductions of life has to remind us of the technique in films, with their capacity to sum up history or a life in an hour or two. Interestingly, the most common root meaning of the word "play" in many different languages is *rapid movement*. Play is likened to flickering like flames, fluttering like birds, leaping like animals, bobbing like a ship on the waves. Here perhaps also lies a part of the reason for the vividness of play—its quickness in action. Apparently throughout history players have always made their own action movies.

Just as the players show their first efforts at self-control in play, they likewise show their first efforts at abstraction. Babies' blowing bubbles is the first abstraction. It is the first removal of themselves from the usual flow of sucking, and it is a restatement of parts of that flow.

It also follows that because children are in charge of the circumstances, the more they repeat these play events, the more they will be likely to introduce novelty into their activity. Given that they originally intend to reverse the direction of power and to make their own imprint on nature and society, it follows that with repetition that uniqueness will become increasingly apparent; that is, the more children play (all other things being equal), the more playful they should become. If they do not become playful, this is because they are too obsessed with the difficulties in their life. Thus, we find that in therapy disturbed children repeat the same themes endlessly in their attempt to gain freedom from them. They smash the adult dolls a thousand times before they begin to feel some freedom. In due course, however, this play does lead to some feeling of such freedom.

But in normal children each attempt to deal with the irreversible problem of being powerless can only be enjoyable if the problem is stated in a novel way. In play there is the freedom for such novelty. Without novelty the play itself would become boring. Thus, there is an inherent drive toward statements about life that are unique.

We should find in play, therefore, unique syntheses of the way life might be. When children put a doll to bed at age eighteen months, they give us a forecast of many later events. It will be another year before they can talk about such things, however. Representation in play is much easier than is representation in speech. In play children just have to put the action elements of representation together (the doll, the bed, and the putting into bed). In speech children have to use the words "I put the baby to bed" (not just the actions), and they have to talk to other people and make them understand them. This is much more complex.

When children get to be four, they will be able to put a real baby to bed, as four-year-olds often have to do in tribal living. But the play statement of this event comes first. It forecasts all the rest. Of course, this is not a very unique example. For children who play a lot, putting the baby to bed gets to be putting it under the bed, putting a teddy bear to bed, putting baby and teddy to bed, turning the bed upside down and making a house out of it, and using the bed as a boat or as an airplane. This is the way in which the uniqueness becomes increasingly manifest, although even the personal statement is unique at least for that individual.

Out of the uniqueness of the play abstraction comes children's capacity to be creative. It is because they have developed a repertoire of novel ideas that they can give novel responses to the usual creativity tests. This is the inherent connection between play and creativity.

GAMES

We can define play as that reversal of the direction of power that permits unique abstracts of life to be experienced in a vivid manner and subsequently recorded as fun. Games work within these limits but deal only with the problem of interactions between people. The play problem they have in mind is the character of relations between people. They attempt to digest into capsule form what we have called the fitting positions of chaser and escapee, acceptor and rejector, etc.

In our judgment each of these fitting sets of positions represents a learning of conflict. One must know how to accept and reject because without a lot of experience on any given occasion we may not know which to do. Life is full of acceptances and rejections, and we must be ready for them. It seems clear that games do not deal with all kinds of interaction. They deal primarily with interactions that involve oppositions. A game is an opposition between players.

The types of oppositions that games deal with are three-fold. There is the opposition between order and disorder, which we dealt with in Chapter 8, and oppositions that have to do with approach and avoidance and with success and failure, which we have dealt with in subsequent chapters. Let us take approach and avoidance first. We have to learn how to relate to people. Shall we go toward them or shall we go away from them? If we go toward them, should it be as pursuit; if we go away, should it be as escape? Alternatively, should we simply accept them or reject them, be dominated by them or usurp their role, and more dangerously should we attack them or defend ourselves against them? It is possible to group together games of these types and show that there is a steady development through each type. This is what we have been doing in the previous pages.

Likewise, we have attempted to show that there are games in which the main opposition has to do with success and failure. We have mentioned the opposition between being correct and making mistakes. There is also the opposition between scoring or being outscored, as in most games of skill. We have not given much time to the other type of success or failure, that which occurs in games of chance. We see this as an opposition between accumulating goods or being deprived of them by virtue of lady luck or other external agencies over which we do not have control.

The original games of order and disorder often have the players combining together against anarchy or fate, so if we are to include them in a definition of games, we must talk of games as involving an opposition between forces (not always between players). This then covers solitaire and individual gaming. Without the cooperative behavior established through these order games, games of opposition between players could not take place, since all competition presupposes that the players can first cooperate on the meaning of the rules.

The way we visualize the hierarchy of games through which children develop is as follows:

Games of *order and disorder* ("Ring around the Rosy")
Games of *approach and avoidance*
Chasing and escaping (tag)
Acceptance and rejection ("The Farmer in the Dell")
Dominance and usurpation (Mother may I)
Attack and defense (football, chess)
Games of *success and failure*
Accumulation and deprivation (bingo)
Correctness or mistakes (jump rope)
Scoring or being outscored (marbles)

A game then becomes an opposition between forces with an uncertain outcome and with rules controlling the character of the events. As in play, in the game the players control the circumstances and have the power over their fate that they may not have outside of games; they are vividly absorbed into action and interaction; and the game is a unique abstract of the larger texture of social life. It presents to children a simple pattern of the way people manage opposition many years before they will be able to handle adroitly that opposition in the larger society.

It is interesting to realize that each type of game has a special flavor of life. Think of kissing in the ring, Monopoly, checkers, dodge ball, and Red Rover. One can think of things in life that are like these events. Nothing quite parallels them of course, but each is a metaphor for how it will be with other people. The images of these games become the basis for our less sophisticated expectations of other people.

Furthermore, when we play each game, it is different every time we play it, which is probably itself the best preparation for what is to come. Even within each theme each encounter has a different quality. As we proceed in games, we get unique strategies for managing them, so that although the content of the game opposition may be changed little by us, we do have latitude for our own particular style. In play novelty of ideas can affect content. In games it seems to have its main effect on style. Games are thus vehicles of the major culture in a way that play has a chance not to be, although, as we have seen, play's major contents are usually repetitive of everyday themes.

RELATIONSHIP OF PLAY TO SOCIETY

We play for power, for our own "abstract" and vivid statement. But what relationship does all this have to the rest of society? All the evidence shows that play *reproduces that society*. Children's play is full of the content of their lives. Eskimos constantly play at turn-taking skill games without competition because they must both know each other's skills and yet collaborate together. When they are on the ice floe with a polar bear working as a team, it must be one-for-all and all-for-one, but with a keen sense of each other's competence.

Aboriginal play imitates tracking and hunting. Games of strategy arise in human history at the same time as does class stratification, including the formation of military specialists. In societies where monarchical rule is the form of social order children and adults play games in which one person tries to be king over all the others. An example from Afghanistan follows:

The king of Afghanistan sat on a brocade-covered sofa and sipped tea as he watched some of the fiercest, most agile horsemen in Central Asia play a form of mounted football with the carcass of a beheaded calf.

This gentle pastime is played here every year at this time in honor of the birthday of the king, Mohammed Zahir Shah, who has now turned 54.

To score in the game—known as buzkashi—all a rider has to do is snatch the carcass from the ground, gallop with it a quarter of a mile down the field, then gallop back and throw it in a chalked circle near the point where he started.

Grabbing the carcass can be a bit tricky, however, for it weighs 75 to 100 pounds. Also, at the moment the rider leans from his saddle to hoist this weight, several of his opponents' powerful horses are likely to come slamming into his in an attempt to knock the carcass loose.

For a moment the men and animals shove and heave like a wave on the verge of breaking. Then with shouts and a cracking of whips, one of the horsemen breaks loose from the pack at a hard gallop, somehow throwing a leg over the heavy carcass to hold it to the side of his mount.

At that instant buzkashi has more than a touch of epic beauty as the horsemen stretch out across the landscape in thunderous pursuit.

Often, when the lead rider is caught, a tug-of-war results with the carcass stretched between two galloping horses, their riders leaning away at angles of 45 degrees or more to break the opponent's hold.

That's how buzkashi gets its name. Kashi means pull and buz means goat, calves being only one of several possibilities for the carcass.

The buzkashi matches sponsored here by the National Olympic Federation for His Majesty's pleasure are as rugged and dangerous a sport spectacle as can be seen anywhere—except on the far side of the mountain barrier called the Hindu Kush, near the Soviet border, where Turkmen and Uzbek horsemen play it without any reference to the rule book the Olympic Federation has attempted to write.

Here there are ten men on a side playing on a field with marked boundaries under the supervision of a referee who is supposed to call a foul if one of the players uses such traditional buzkashi tactics as whipping an opponent across the face or pulling him from his horse.

In the north, there can be 100 men on a side or, so it is said, there can even be no sides at all—each man pitted against the rest. That sounds like certain death, but apparently it isn't for the best horsemen, called chapandaz, survive to play for the King on his birthday.

One of today's stars, Hakim Pahlavon, has only half of one ear, a minor example of the kinds of injuries a chapandaz can sustain.[1]

This is "monarchical" play at its richest. This play remains with us only in the diminished form of king of the mountain. A new pattern of games has taken its place.

In twentieth-century American society, with its greater emphasis on individual achievement, we play games in which all the players score and record their achievements in complicated statistics of batting, pitching, and errors. In more-recent

[1] *The New York Times,* October 24, 1968, p. 49.

corporate America we play games that reflect the massive powers and strategies of large organizations, as in American football.

Just as play and games reproduce aspects of the societies in which they take place, so also do they tend to reflect the character of their players. We know from research that chess players tend to be disputatious, solitary individuals; that some types of bridge players tend to be gregarious people who prefer not to discuss serious issues; that people attracted to team sports tend to be more aggressive than are those attracted to individual athletic endeavors; and that even winning child tic-tac-toe players tend to be strategic-thinking individuals, and those who prefer to draw in tic tac toe are more cautious and less risk-taking in character.

So what does society get? This research implies that in play or games the individual or the group takes one of society's themes and reproduces it either uniquely or with their own style of play. Reproducing the theme in this way, under one's own control and with the vivid engrossment involved, means that one restates the main themes of personal and cultural life without the usual irritations and harassments that surround them. What this leads to is a *regeneration of cultural purposes*, a revival. The players or gamesters return from their episodes more confident and optimistic about their usual lives. Play and games recharge the batteries of their customary selves.

Furthermore, because this has been an exercise in novelty with respect to these purposes, it is possible that they may also gain new insight into the way things might be. At least life has been restated in personal terms without all the other problems it contains, and that in itself sometimes leads to a shift in perspective and an easing of the original problems. Typically, the participants in play therapy or psychodrama return to their original problem with a new self-consciousness, a new ability to laugh at circumstances. Businessmen return from their sport with a new insight into their own affairs.

In short, play, games, and sports promote *reflection* as well as *regeneration,* and this is probably what we have always meant when we said that they are reviving. Reviving means regeneration and reflection. We vive in order to revive.

IDEOLOGIES OF PLAY

In promoting the view that viving revives whether in play, games, or sports, we have run head on into the problem that most people do not believe this. For the past several centuries the prevailing view has been that play and games are trivial. Now this is an exceptional view. Throughout history most peoples have highly valued their states of play, which they have associated with their religion and their ritual. Thus, we have to explain what caused this devaluation of play and games to occur in our own historical times.

Our explanation for this is that the Industrial Revolution, which needed people as cogs in factory machinery and as clerks in sales departments, had to force a predominantly rural European culture from its festive and seasonal way of life. The notion that work was supreme and that play was evil was an ideological doctrine that helped to provide the Industrial Revolution with the human machinery that it needed. It brought the rural workers from the farms and kept the clerks at their desks. For obvious reasons we call this the *"Scroogian"* ideology of play. It is also known as the work ethic.

While the workers were being put in their place in the nineteenth century, however, the leisure classes were being as idle as their money would allow. Under the guise of amateurism they maintained a flexible grasp of the keys to the kingdom.

Modern forms of such "amateurism" are the expense account and the think tank, within which the ruling classes in the midst of their "play" get to reflect on the matters of power and to regenerate their own desire to continue controlling it.

A review of the economist John Maynard Keynes' book *Essays in Biography* in *The New York Times* points out that "It is one of the pleasant ironies of history that a man who with his fellows pretended to live only for intellectual, sensory and aesthetic pleasures . . . should have done more than any other to rescue millions from economic misery. . . . He would pursue truth even if it took him to hell and back."[2] He did not, he said, believe in working more than an hour a day. This is the *Keynsian* ideology of play.

Modern affluence means that we all are Keynsians in our own way. We all have time to spare to consider and reconsider the character of our lives. More of us are also required to be creative to be successful and to be flexible to keep up with changing conditions. Such versatility is promoted by the notion that play serves as well as work in this world of ours.

The role reversal of play and games seems to be the factor that contributes to flexibility. The unique personal abstracts of play and cultural abstracts of games seem to be bases for their contribution to novelty and creativity. Finally, it is the vivification of the experience itself that returns us to our ordinary ways with a feeling of regeneration and revival. We hope that play with your own children will be sufficiently fun filled so that it also becomes as much a vive for you as it does for them.

2 *The New York Times*, January 2, 1973, p. 33.

Appendix:

Assessment

We have made innumerable suggestions in this book about how to play with children and how children play among or by themselves. In this appendix we have set down an inventory of this behavior. This provides you with a check list against which to consider the range of both your own playfulness and your child's playfulness. Naturally this is a limited list. It covers only those things that we have dealt with here. There is much more. Different families have different styles, and they add new elements to their playful life.

Still, the value of this behavior inventory is that it helps to show that development through play is systematic. It tries to indicate the paths along which you can help children to travel and can expect them to travel. In addition, it provides a guide and a key for your own games with them. Perhaps the most important way children become versatile is by having parents model the kind of versatility advocated in these chapters. The inventory provides you with a form of self-assessment— although we should point out that scoring yourself in this way is only one sort of game. One superb piece of fun may be better than a dozen dribbling examples.

We also provide an inventory of the children's play. This covers all the types of play we have dealt with, including solitary and social play, exploration, testing, imitation, and construction, as well as representation and dramatics. Under dramatics we add the various *dynamics* without which drama would not be possible. Here again is a brief assessment of what you can expect in your children's behavior year by year.

BIRTH TO THREE MONTHS
1. Imitate baby, make baby noises
2. Alternate noises with baby (gurgles)
3. "Baby talk" (long vowels and high pitch)
4. Make clown faces
5. Bicycle, push baby's legs
6. Poke out your tongue
7. Dance with baby in your arms
8. Sing to baby
9. Put your finger in baby's mouth
10. Chew baby's hand
11. Let baby pull your pinky
12. Play Bob-White (long low sound and sudden high note)

THREE TO SIX MONTHS
1. Make baby laugh (vary regular behavior)
2. Do gymnastics with baby (bounce on bed, turn upside down, toss in air)
3. Babble at baby
4. Blow raspberries on baby's body
5. Tickle baby
6. Fall over, clown for baby's laughter
7. Bounce baby on your knee
8. Play knee games ("Ride a Cock Horse")
9. Play "pretend" walking, "pretend" standing
10. Let baby pull your hair
11. Play "This Little Pig"
12. Play "There Was a Little Mouse"
13. Play "Pat-a-Cake"
14. Sing "Rock-a-Bye Baby"

SIX TO TWELVE MONTHS
1. Suck on baby's fingers
2. Practice mock falling, hang baby upside down
3. Roughhouse
4. Play one, two, three, and up
5. Grab and give up (give and take)

6. Play peek-a-boo (locate object or person)
7. Bury baby under blanket
8. Play hear-a-boo (locate sound)
9. Crackle newspapers
10. Chase dog
11. Ride camel
12. Make funny faces
13. Make mirror faces
14. Play book peek-a-boo
15. Make baby laugh (sound, touch, social, and visual stimuli)

ONE TO TWO YEARS
1. Chase, be chased (one at a time)
2. Hide thimble
3. Play peep-oh
4. Pretend to lose things (and people)
5. Do hugging greetings
6. Toss baby
7. Empty, fill
8. Play catch
9. Play body games
10. Retrieve
11. Pretend disapproval
12. Play phony birthdays
13. Have tug-of-war
14. Do "Here Is a Beehive"
15. Play "Which Hand?"
16. Do "Knock at the Door"
17. Do "Hey Johnny"

TWO TO THREE YEARS
1. Enter into pretense
2. Reverse roles, be powerless one
3. Exaggerate helplessness
4. Report on "their" past, share "reports"
5. Switch roles in chasing

6. Watch performer (gymnast, dancer, singer)
7. Play ring games ("Ring around the Rosy")
8. Do group imitations together of everyday events (washing)
9. They hide it, you find it
10. Misname pictures
11. Tell stories to be filled in, act out scenarios
12. Play follow the leader
13. Guess what it is
14. Smash things

THREE TO FOUR YEARS

1. Reverse roles (child as parent, parent as child)
2. Tell stories together in dialogue form
3. Act out fairy tales
4. Practice motor routines with card and board games
5. Play hide and seek
6. Have pretend telephone conversations
7. Be dumb racer
8. Participate in make-believe

FOUR TO FIVE YEARS

1. Play games of courage
2. Do group pantomiming (animals)
3. Use hand puppets (with different voices)
4. Do story reversals (story idiocy)
5. Be skilled mimic
6. Engage in celebrations

FIVE TO SEVEN YEARS

1. Listen to, and play with, dreams
2. Tell "what if" stories
3. Improvise movements
4. Improvise objects
5. Improvise characters doing routine things
6. Improvise imaginary situations

7. Improvise feelings
8. Improvise imaginary people
9. Improvise gullibility and buffoonery

SEVEN TO NINE YEARS

1. Play "ham"
2. Play referee
3. Play with skill
4. Improvise exaggerated characters
5. Be "riddler"
6. Play with double meanings
7. Indulge nonsense
8. Relate loony collections
9. Teach magic tricks
10. Suggest crazy drawings
11. Play guessing games
12. Play car games

NINE TO THIRTEEN YEARS

1. Ask "What did it look like, what did it feel like?"
2. Improvise imaginary interactions
3. Improvise conflict
4. Improvise psychodramas (be several people)
5. Dramatize: realism, moralism, technique, feeling, and empathy
6. Play theater games
7. Encourage creative writing, poetry
8. Make up game simulations, constructions
9. Play sandlot sports

II: *What They Can Do* *Check*

BIRTH TO THREE MONTHS

1. Engage in mouth play
2. Engage in hand play
3. Engage in sound play (vocal play)
4. Respond to your stimulus (sound) by repetition
5. Show surprise at your stimulus (face or sound)

THREE TO SIX MONTHS
  1. Play with food
  2. Play with nipple
  3. Engage in recognition play (excitement at familiar things)
  4. Experience excitement (mobiles)
  5. Engage in object play (toys)
  6. Engage in power play (create effects)
  7. Move in rhythm with you
  8. "Sing" with you
  9. Laugh at your incongruities
  10. Anticipate crescendo of excitement in cumulative games
       ("This Little Pig")

SIX TO TWELVE MONTHS
  1. Exploratory play (with basic forces)
       bang
       insert, poke
       twist, turn
       push, pull
       crawl under
       get into
       open, shut (in, out)
       climb (in, out, up, down)
       squeeze
       drop
  2. Enjoyment of vertigo
  3. Dramatics
       imitate novel stimuli (try new sounds or faces)
       anticipate climax
       be delighted at outcome
       make you audience
       appear, reappear

ONE TO TWO YEARS
  1. Exploration (specific to object)
       hammer (peg board)
       empty, fill (containers with toys)

open, shut (doors)
roll (ball)
crayon
separate (play dough)

2. Construction
   connect objects together (threading, train)
   disjoint objects (separate linked objects)
   stack, knock down (blocks)
   relate objects (doll in car, train on rail)
   group similar objects (dishes, blocks)

3. Testing (exercise of player, not necessarily specific object)
   run
   throw
   jump
   climb
   pedal
   hit
   balance
   dance
   retrieve
   march
   hide
   search
   lose
   find

4. Social testing (with other children)
   watch others
   cuddle others
   hit others
   exchange with others
   run or stand with others
   play either being chased or chasing with elders

5. Imitation (which is now also solitary representation)
   imitate own or others' actions
       pretend to sleep
       pretend to wash
       pretend to eat
   transform objects into toy subjects
       sand becomes water

      stone becomes boat
      cookie becomes animal
      safety pin is grandmother
      doll is baby
      teddy bear is daddy
   make toys carry out actions
      doll drinks from cup
      teddy bear drinks from cup
      doll sleeps, drinks, cries, washes

6. Dramatics (Dramatics of prior year are repeated; namely, surprise, anticipation, excitement, crescendo, delight at outcome, appearance and disappearance, making you audience.)
   make entrances, exits, with performance (dance)
   personify (pretend to sleep)
   do pretense interactions (mock disapproval)
   practice expressions ("hi," "good-bye")

Two to Three Years

1. Exploration and construction
   make constructions with blocks (houses)
   combine materials (blocks, toys, clay)
   mold and name objects (animals, food)
   use tools (clay, wood, scissors, hammers, knives)
   finger paint, poster paint, scribble
   do puzzles

2. Testing
   climb
   hop on one foot
   balance on beam
   throw ball
   hang by arms
   roll down hill
   somersault
   jump from low heights

3. Social testing (to sustain play group)
   solicit adult help with other children
   use physical force with others

II: *What They Can Do* (continued)   *Check*

use strategy (make offers, bargains)
block (negation, prevention)
seek inclusion, exclude others
be bossy
4. Imitation and representation (solitary)
carry out actions on toys
doll is put to bed
doll is fed with spoon
make toys carry out action on toys (complete sequence
of action is now represented, instead of only parts of
actions)
teddy bear feeds doll
give running commentary and show awareness of pretense
child explains why teddy bear feeds doll
become play actors themselves (Prior to this they were
silent manipulators behind scenes.)
child is parent and feeds babies (dolls)
represent sequence of events in time
parent feeds, undresses, and puts baby to bed
engage in gamelike counter interaction, which develops
with pretense
parent (child) has to spank naughty child (doll)
5. Dramatics
personify routines of adult (parent)
change roles (from hider to seeker), although not flexibly
play along in choral group games
continue narrative in stories
"perform" (dance, somersault)

THREE TO FOUR YEARS
1. Exploration and construction
engage in verbal exploration (ask "why?")
engage in intellectual exploration (make rules)
make visits (by train, bus)
explore immediate neighborhood
make music (percussion and the like) in time
play sorting and matching games (with buttons, coins)
cut paper, match designs
explore plants, animals, trees

make houses (with blocks, blankets, boxes)
construct toy worlds—people and things (with dolls, trucks, soldiers)
show new interest in their "paintings" as products
2. Testing
climb jungle gyms
walk line heel to toe
catch ball with arm outstretched
throw ball ten feet
3. Social testing and play
engage in simple contagion play (imitate each other)
play in simple unison (all do same things at same time —rhythm)
take turns
    alternate same behavior
    alternate different but repeated behavior
    alternate new behaviors
engage in central-person play (one dominates)
run from imaginary central persons (witches)
organize play around common themes (house play)
play follow the leader
4. Imitation and representation (solitary)
personify characters with feelings, represent emotions (anger, crying)
make spatial differentiations in playing area (Kitchen, bedroom, gas station are differentiated.)
portray multiple characters interacting (Dyads—parent and child—are most typical, but siblings and others are added.)
represent agencies independently (Miniature play worlds of cars, soldiers, houses, and the like, begin to play more-conventional role.)
5. Dramatics
portray characters with feeling
show concern for different situations or settings (home, shop) in imaginative play
take role of parent and baby
engage in play conversation via telephone
act out fairy tale plots
participate in narrative fairy tales

II: *What They Can Do* (continued)   *Check*

FOUR TO FIVE YEARS

1. Exploration and construction

    sort and match school-type materials (colors, shapes, pictures)

    have secrets, surprises

    watch insects, beetles

    play with packing cases, boxes

    enjoy boats, airplanes, country or town excursions

    notice odors (skunk, onion), tastes (sassafras, berries)

    look at books

    play with tinker toys, Lego, cutting out, pasting, log sticks

2. Testing

    swim

    roller skate

    ride scooter

    catch ball with elbows at side

    fall over, whirl around

    ride vehicles (go-cart)

    engage in music and movement

    hop on one foot

    bounce tennis ball

3. Social testing and play

    play games of order and disorder ("Ring around the Rosy")

    engage in group play fantasies (imitate television themes) with different roles

    establish play rituals (possessions, sequences)

    have friends and enemies (boys and girls)

    play with puppets

    change roles in hide and seek and in chasing (now done with routine skill)

4. Imitation and representation

    become imaginary character (monster, clown)

    anticipate future events (plan party or whatever for Christmas; previously time was shown only by sequencing of events.)

    differentiate space into two types of territory—safe and dangerous places

5. Dramatics
   adopt different roles (with puppets, in imaginary play)
   use different voices (for puppets)
   invent story narrative (change old narrative)

FIVE TO SEVEN YEARS
1. Exploration and construction
   explore territory (parks, beaches)
   begin collections (leaves, stones)
   play city games (elaborate sand-pit worlds with several
       locations and toy vehicles linking them)
   use magnets, magnifying glasses, compass
   use mats, potholders
   do simple weaving, sewing
   do clay modeling with tools
   play at being boys, girls, and babies (sex)
   play with doll clothing and doll houses
   make costumes
   play with toy farms, forts, castles
   use coloring books
   look at comics
2. Testing
   use rope ladder, trapeze, stilts
   skate, skip
   swim
   swing, seesaw
   play with tires
3. Social testing and play
   display role flexibility, shift high- and low-powered roles in
       informal play
   adopt fitting roles (seller-buyer, teacher-pupil)
   play games of acceptance and rejection ("The Farmer in
       the Dell")
   play games of pursuit and escape (chasing)
   play games of attack and defense (running)
   have playful conversations

4. Imitation, representation, and dramatics
   improvise movements, objects, characters, situations, imaginary situations, feelings, imaginary people
   make up episodic plots

Seven to Nine Years

1. Exploration and construction
   play with mechanical trains, mechanical cars
   play with Barbie dolls (plus accessories) and paper dolls, dress up
   use stick puppets
   use hammers, pliers, saws, braces
   keep collections (cards, covers)
   determine animal sex differences
   show interest in bees, butterflies, pollination
2. Testing
   ride two-wheeled bicycles
3. Social testing
   resist high power figures (release)
   play games of dominance and usurpation (Mother may I)
   be concerned with correctness or mistakes (jump rope)
   play dominoes, checkers, card and board games
   play games of attack and defense (with some wrestling)
   play sandlot baseball, touch football
   swap possessions
4. Imitation, representation, and dramatics
   improvise exaggerated characters
   improvise nonsense
   perform group stunts, dramas (circuses, TV)
   make up cumulative plots

Nine to Thirteen Years

1. Exploration and construction
   use workbench
   do handicrafts
   put models together
   do weaving, woodworking, metalwork, bookbinding, leatherwork, carving, basketry

visit museums, factories
do creative writing
construct games
2. Testing
   go camping
   do outdoor exploring (streams, beaches)
3. Social testing and games (In summarizing shifts in games between six and twelve years, we stress change from transitory to definite winning and losing outcomes; from episodic, through cumulative and climactic, to regular time intervals; from indirect contact [tagging, marbles, balls] to direct physical contact; from unequal high and lower power roles, through role exchange based on skill, to specialized roles [as in sports]; and from diffuse to organized teams.)

   play sandlot sports
   do intellectual games (Scrabble, charades)
   improvise psychodramas
   play theater games
   put on informal concerts
   play games of chasing and escaping (with climax)
   become concerned with success and failure (with definite outcomes)
   play games of attack and defense (with forceful exchange)
4. Imitation, representation, and improvisation
   improvise interactions between characters
   improvise conflict
   engage in open-ended improvisational contests

Index

267